27

D0930739

A Different Language

A
DIFFERENT
LANGUAGE
GERTRUDE STEIN'S
EXPERIMENTAL WRITING

Marianne DeKoven

The University of Wisconsin Press

MIDDLEBURY COLLEGE LIBRARY

PS
3537
.T323
Z586
1983

5/1984
Am. Lit.

Published 1983

The University of Wisconsin Press
114 North Murray Street
Madison, Wisconsin 53715

The University of Wisconsin Press, Ltd.
1 Gower Street
London WC1E 6HA, England

Copyright © 1983
The Board of Regents of the University of Wisconsin System
All rights reserved

First printing

Printed in the United States of America

For LC CIP information see the colophon

ISBN 0-299-09210-0

The excerpt from Journey into the Self: Being the Letters, Papers and Journals of Leo Stein, *edited by Edmund Fuller, are courtesy of Crown Publishers, Inc. Copyright 1950 by the Estate of Leo D. Stein. Reprinted by permission of Crown Publishers, Inc.*

The four short works by Gertrude Stein are from the eight-volume Yale Edition of the Unpublished Writings of Gertrude Stein *edited by Carl Van Vechten: "Rue de Rennes," in* Two: Gertrude Stein and Her Brother, *copyright 1951 by Yale University Press; "Exceptional Conduct" and "Amaryllis or the Prettiest of Legs," in* Bee Time Vine, *copyright 1953 by Yale University Press; and "Duchesse de Rohan" in* Painted Lace, *copyright 1955 by Yale University Press. Reprinted by permission of Yale University Press.*

"Susie Asado" and "A Curtain Raiser" from Geography and Plays, *quotations from Gertrude Stein's unpublished notebooks, and facsimile reproduction of Gertrude Stein's unpublished manuscript pages from "Portrait of Mabel Dodge at the Villa Curonia," "Rue de Rennes," and "Portrait of Constance Fletcher" are courtesy of the Collection of American Literature, Beinecke Rare Book and Manuscript Library, Yale University.*

For Julien

Many words spoken to me have seemed English

Contents

Acknowledgments

I would like to express my deep gratitude to the people who helped me, not only in writing this book but in acquiring the interests and ideas which generated it. I am particularly grateful to Albert Guerard, my dissertation director, mentor, and primary role model. It was from him that I learned to take the avant-garde as seriously as I do. He has given me support, friendship, and example: the example of his eclectic, flexible, nondogmatic approach to literature, and the example of his work, which taught me that the discipline of critical writing *is* the discipline of critical thought.

The Stanford English Department — and specifically its modern literature faculty — was a rich source of friendship and excellent teaching, particularly in the persons of William Chace, Larry Friedlander, Albert Gelpi, Diane Middlebrook, Thomas Moser, and Rob Polhemus. Larry Friedlander and Diane Middlebrook also helped me a great deal in the earliest stages of writing this book, which began as my doctoral dissertation.

For the later stages, I am extremely grateful for the help given me by Elizabeth Abel, Linda Bamber, Marjorie Berger, and, especially, Barbara Cohn Schlachet. They saw exactly what was wrong, and exactly how to make it right. I am also extremely grateful to my colleagues at Rutgers, particularly Maurice Charney, Alice Crozier, Dan Howard, Bridget Lyons, Fred Main, Alicia Ostriker, John Richetti, Elaine Showalter, and Andrew Welsh, who have helped me in more ways than I can enumerate. My husband, Julien Hennefeld, has always been willing to listen and to give thoughtful advice. My son, Daniel Hennefeld, has kept me cheerful, and my mother, Annabel DeKoven, has given me unflagging encouragement. I am grateful for their love and involvement.

I would also like to thank Mary Wyer and Elizabeth Steinberg of the University of Wisconsin Press for their support and interest; Edith Poor for her editing; and Ursula Dafeldecker, Margaret Glassman, and Thomas Bechtle, for their help in preparing the manuscript.

Finally, I would like to thank the Rutgers University Research Council for the Junior Faculty Fellowship which, in large measure, allowed me to complete this book.

Portions of chapter 1 appeared in different form in "Gertrude Stein and Modern Painting: Beyond Literary Cubism," *Contemporary Literature* 22:1 (Winter 1981). Portions of chapter 7 appeared in different form in "Gertrude Stein's Landscape Writing," *Women's Studies* 9:3 (Summer 1982).

Introduction

In this book I argue for the importance of Gertrude Stein's experimental writing—her work after *Three Lives* (1906) and before *The Autobiography of Alice B. Toklas* (1932). I argue for its importance not as influence, though it is important in that way, but as exemplum of a culturally alternative language. I use the term "experimental" for this radical writing, rather than "modernist," "postmodern," or "avant-garde," to emphasize the fact that it violates and reshapes not just the conventions of literature, as modern, postmodern, and avant-garde works have done, but, in addition, the conventions of language itself.

Stein's work from 1906 to 1932 is the most substantial and successful body of experimental writing in English. As a "different language" it both disrupts conventional modes of signification and provides alternatives to them. The modes Stein disrupts are linear, orderly, closed, hierarchical, sensible, coherent, referential, and heavily focused on the signified. The modes she substitutes are incoherent, open-ended, anarchic, irreducibly multiple, often focused on what Roland Barthes calls the "magic of the signifier." I would call conventional writing, insofar as it excludes the modes of signification Stein substitutes, the privileged language of patriarchy. Experimental writing such as Stein's therefore liberates the "different" (*différent*) modes of signification which this privileged patriarchal language has repressed. (I use "patriarchy" in its anthropological sense; according to their structures of kinship and heredity, all existing societies are patriarchal.) Chapter 1 develops these ideas. Chapters 2–7 give a chronological analysis of Gertrude Stein's experimental styles between *Three Lives* (1903–06) and *Stanzas in Meditation* (1932), focusing on the culturally oppositional features of the writing. It is by paying attention to those features that we gain the readiest and the most rewarding access to Stein's experimental work.

As a whole, then, this book arises from four converging aims: (1) to make a case for the importance of experimental writing as an alternative, anti-patriarchal language; (2) to analyze Gertrude Stein's experimental *oeuvre* both as an end in itself and as a varied, complex, largely successful exemplum of anti-patriarchal writing; (3) to chart Stein's successive experimental styles; and (4) to make her hitherto largely inaccessible and unread work accessible and readable.

In Chapter 1, and throughout the book, I use the term "experimental writing" in a fixed rather than a historically relative sense. Much literature and art that we have assimilated as "classic," inside the cultural mainstream, was considered revolutionary, impossible, beyond the pale in its day. However, just as the term "avant-garde" can have either a historically relative or a fixed definition — it can designate either anything that seems or seemed outlandish now or at any time in the past, or it can refer to a specific twentieth-century cultural phenomenon ("*the* avant-garde") — the term "experimental" can be used to designate a specific kind of twentieth-century writing, as I use it here, even though it can be used in a historically relative way as well, to designate any writing considered experimental in its day (*Joseph Andrews, Lyrical Ballads*). Specifically, I have labeled "experimental" that writing which violates grammatical convention, thereby preventing normal reading. This definition is intentionally narrower than the common usage of "experimental." Generally, "experimental" is interchangeable with literary designations such as "avant-garde," "innovative," "modernist" and "postmodern," "anti-realist," "fabulist," "anti-traditional," or "countercultural." I needed a label for the kind of writing which is the subject of this book, and no such generally accepted label exists. I have annexed the term "experimental," in lieu of a coinage, because its connotations make it particularly appropriate to my concerns.

Chapters 2–7 move through Stein's work chronologically, following the course of her successive experimental styles. The division of her work into chronological styles is much more meaningful than the division into works or genres. My aim in these six chapters, with the exception of the chapter on *Three Lives*, is not to interpret specific works, partly because interpretation defeats experimental writing (since it has no Meaning, no unitary coherence), and partly because the division within any experimental style into specific works is generally arbitrary, and often meaningless. What requires analysis, therefore, is the style rather than the work. Accordingly, I choose to analyze in each chapter texts, or fragments of texts, which I find representative of their style.

As a result of my nearly exclusive focus on experimental writing, and on styles rather than works, the organization and weighting of my analyses do not reflect the importance generally now accorded various works in the Stein canon. The chronological limits I've set exclude *The Autobiography of Alice B. Toklas, Everybody's Autobiography, The Geographical History of America, Mrs. Reynolds, Ida,* the late operas and plays, *Wars I Have Seen, Brewsie and Willie,* and the other important works of the thirties and forties. To the extent that those works are experimental, they employ linguistic modes Stein developed in the "landscape" writing of the twenties.

But even within the experimental period, I do not give readings, as such, of *The Making of Americans, GMP, Many Many Women, A Long Gay Book, Two, Tender Buttons,* "Lifting Belly," any of the famous portraits, *How To Write,* or *Stanzas in Meditation.* I do not believe that the writing collected under any of those titles constitutes a "work," in the way we normally understand that word: a coherent literary unit, separate and distinguishable from any other, which it is the critic's task to account for as a whole. However, I hope that my analyses elucidate the writing lodged under those titles, along with other writing not considered as important, by elucidating Stein's experimental writing at what is — *for that writing* — the most inclusive, defining level: the level of style.

Although Stein never intended to be anti-patriarchal (any more than Richardson, Defoe, or Fielding intended to invent a literary genre for the rising bourgeoisie), opposition to patriarchal modes seems to me the ultimate *raison d'être* for all experimental writing. While it is not necessary to make that assertion in order to read or criticize experimental writing, it does seem to me necessary to do so in order to account for its existence and importance in twentieth-century Western culture. The first chapter aims at such an account, using in part what has been the most helpful terminology for the purpose: that of current French feminist, poststructuralist, and psychoanalytic criticism. This terminology has been particularly helpful because of its emphasis on the interplay of language and culture. I use that terminology (signifier, signified, signification, symbolic and presymbolic, logocentric and phallogocentric, *différence* [though not *différance*], *jouissance*, patriarchal and anti-patriarchal, Oedipal and pre-Oedipal, pluridimensional, polysemous) only to treat the large cultural and political implications of the subversions which experimental writing enacts. The terminology therefore appears in concentrated form only in Chapter 1. It reappears intermittently throughout the rest of the book, when I want to remind the reader of the cultural import of the observations I make about patterns of signification in Stein's writing; but on the whole, Chapters 2–7 assume the cultural generalizations of Chapter 1 without mentioning them very often.

The "French terminology" works best for distant looking — for standing back to get the large picture of language, of writing, in relation to such vast entities as the psyche, gender, Western civilization, and civilization in general. I begin with that kind of distant looking in order to establish the abstract framework which gives significance to the closer looking that follows. For the purposes of that closer looking — for taking a phrase, sentence, or paragraph and saying exactly where in it meaning resides, what kind of meaning it is, how language is structured to create it, and how it reaches the reader — the tools and terminology of Anglo-American "close reading" have been most helpful.

Although my analyses of Stein's writing do not depend on the generalizations of Chapter 1 in any direct way, the features of the writing which make it anti-patriarchal — its polysemy, and its presymbolic modes of signification — are precisely the features which determine the methods of reading I employ. And though Derrida is important to the theory in Chapter 1, I do not deconstruct Stein's writing. To do so would be inappropriate and, in fact, impossible. Instead I take it as already deconstructed. It *is* the indeterminate, anti-patriarchal (anti-logocentric, anti-phallogocentric, presymbolic, pluridimensional) writing which deconstruction, alias Jacques Derrida, proposes as an antidote to Western culture, and which Julia Kristeva proposes as an antidote to patriarchy.

The mode of writing I advocate in Chapter 1 is anarchic, undifferentiated, indeterminate, multiple, open-ended; it is opposed to objectivity, order, lucidity, linearity, mastery, and coherence. However, my criticism of Stein in Chapters 2–7 is manifestly coherent, orderly, determinate, linear in the most blatant way, I hope lucid, and aimed quite frankly at mastery of Stein's experimental writing. I do not think practical (as opposed to theoretical) criticism can ever wholly, or more than glancingly, adopt experimental modes without relinquishing its ontological difference from the literary texts it aims to elucidate — something it should not really want to do. I believe that practical criticism exists to elucidate literary texts, and therefore cannot partake of the freedom which is the essence of the literary text. The strategy of this book makes a claim for the possibility of coexistence, even cooperation, between the ideas of *la nouvelle critique* and the methods of Anglo-American positivism.

A similar claim is at the heart of the book itself. In championing anti-patriarchal writing, I do not advocate the elimination of the male modes enthroned by the patriarchy, only the elimination of their tyranny over the female. After all, the modes enthroned by patriarchy have a lot to offer. What kind of intellectual life would we have without reason, order, clarity, determinacy, judgment, abstraction — even the despised mastery, linearity, and dominance of the speaking subject? Ideally, we needn't choose one mode over the other. Both can be available, interpenetrating, opposite only in abstract definition. The area of their juncture can be an open field, whose shape is created by the free activity of the explorer. Neither need be valorized at the expense of the other, neither need be considered a contradiction of the other (it seems we continually struggle in this century against the grip of that supremely simplistic, reductive, life-denying either/or); but rather, each can have its proper sphere, freely available as an alternative to, a complication and correction of, the other.

While my account of experimental writing as anti-patriarchal literature is articulated at the level of culture rather than individual psyche, I do have things to say, at times, about possible connections between Stein's shifting attitude toward her gender and the anti-patriarchal nature of her experimental writing. There is a good deal of unacknowledged anger and bitterness about female experience in *Three Lives*, which seems to vanish as Stein's writing becomes fully experimental. That could well be entirely a result, as is generally now assumed, of her happiness with Alice Toklas. But I hypothesize that it might also be a shift of the rebellious impulse, so troublesome for Stein as content in *Three Lives*, to the structures of language itself. As linguistic structure, the rebellious impulse loses the specifically feminist content it has in *Three Lives*, where women are clearly victims of their culturally determined female virtues. It is mainly women writers who are feminist at the level of thematic content, who write directly, either critically or in celebration, about female experience. But any writer can be anti-patriarchal at the level of linguistic structure: anyone can feel constricted by, and can therefore oppose and remake, the closed, hierarchical, linear, monologistic structures of conventional thought-in-language.

French feminist writers such as Luce Irigaray and Hélène Cixous advocate a "female" language which, in most of its features, is the same as experimental, anti-patriarchal writing as I see it here. They, like some American feminists, consider conventional language to be specifically male as well as patriarchal, citing particularly abstraction, detachment, logical orderliness, mastery, and the dominance of the speaking subject as male linguistic modes. I would differentiate between that kind of gender distinction for language — "male language," "female language" — and the idea of patriarchal and anti-patriarchal language. Conventional language is patriarchal not because it *is* male, but because it exaggerates, hypostatizes, exclusively valorizes male modes of signification, silencing the female presymbolic, pluridimensional modes articulated by experimental writing. These modes are female only because they are pre-Oedipal, not because they constitute a special women's language, any more than male modes constitute a special men's language. Our language is distorted, for all of us, not by the male itself, but by the dominance of the male over the female, the Father over the Mother: conscious over unconscious, symbolic over presymbolic, signified over signifier. We all, except in experimental writing, speak and write patriarchal language. Women's language does diverge in identifiable ways from men's, but those divergences have to do with women's political-historical status in patriarchal society, and with the development of a female tradition in literature — a development which has been established and analyzed in pioneering books such as Elaine Showalter's *A Literature of Their Own* and Sandra Gilbert and Susan Gubar's *The Madwoman in the Attic*. This female literary tradition is different from the presymbolic, pluridimensional "female" as I define it here. Overall, the female literary tradition has enacted its subversions of patriarchy in the realms of content and literary form rather than in the realm of linguistic structure. It is experimental writing that is anti-patriarchal in linguistic structure.

For the purposes of my theoretical argument in Chapter 1, the use of the words "male" and "female" would, in fact, be confusing, because I am discussing linguistic gender abstractions rather than actual men's and women's language. No living person is the embodiment of a gender abstraction, even though those abstractions of gender difference function powerfully in our culture. A "normal" heterosexual male can be an anti-patriarchal writer — he can place himself in opposition to patriarchy — without forfeiting his own particular maleness, which, like any particular woman's femaleness, is always a vastly complicated amalgam of adjustments, compromises, individual circumstances. Experimental writers do not *become* women, they *locate* themselves *in the position of* woman: the opposite of, and antidote to, patriarchal modes of signification.

In fact, most published experimental writing so far has been done by men, and the formal conservatism of the majority of women writers has frequently been remarked. One can only speculate about why that is the case. I subscribe to the theory that it has to do with the insecurity and marginality of women writers. Outsiders must "prove themselves," become acceptable, by adopting, carefully, the style of the dominant culture. Male writers have rebelled from within the security of their natural ownership of the dominant style; women writers, until, literally, now, have been struggling to gain the position which male writers have been free to see as false.

The question of conscious or even unconscious feminist intention is not relevant to my discussion of Stein's writing in "insistence," "lively words," "voices and plays," or "melody," because I am not interested in the particular lexical meanings Stein articulates in those styles. Instead I am interested in how she articulates them, in the linguistic structures which generate and determine meaning. Particular lexical meanings become secondary to the nature and effect of the writing as I perceive it in that period. Whatever explicitly female material there is in that writing, as recent feminist studies have shown, exists at the level of lexical meaning, of content, rather than linguistic structure (although, again, those structures are, at the largest level, anti-patriarchal). But the question of specifically female material, and perhaps feminist intention, does become relevant to the "landscape" writing of the twenties. Thematic content becomes important again in the "landscape" writing; moreover, it articulates a female vision: a vision implied, though not dictated, by the anti-patriarchal linguistic structures of Stein's previous experimental work.

We are not used to talking about linguistic structures as political. We generally restrict political analysis of literature to thematic content, or to those elements of style clearly related to it. We tend also to require, or feel uncomfortable without, evidence of conscious intention on the author's part, particularly for political, cultural analysis of a radical or avant-garde cast. However, such analysis is really no different from discovering attitudes toward the breakup of the feudal order and the rise of the bourgeoisie in Shakespeare, though Shakespeare would never have used such terms, or from discovering unresolved Oedipal feelings in Dickens (or in *Oedipus*). Such analysis seems more acceptable, I think, only because it is more familiar. Whatever uneasiness the reader might feel about calling Stein's writing anti-patriarchal could be dispelled by the increasing familiarity of analyses of the politics of linguistic structure. Such analyses do use terminology and ideas alien to the author whose writing they treat, but no more alien than the terminology and ideas of a great deal of standard contemporary criticism.

Because Stein's writing is so radically *different*, evaluation has always been a problem for her critics. Edmund Wilson's view of Stein in *Axel's Castle* has been extremely influential, and is probably most representative of the general sense of her. He liked *Three Lives;* he liked some of her later work when it was clearly deft and funny; but he lost patience with the radical experimental writing. In general, he thought she was a serious writer, important to Hemingway and Anderson, but a writer who had just gone too far.

Some of her more recent critics claim objectivity in treating her work, or apologize for seeming to defend her. Others dismiss her altogether. Many more *do* defend her. I am in the last camp, but I do not defend all of her. It seems to me the most credible defense is one that distinguishes between what deserves admiration and what perhaps does not. That leads me to make evaluative judgments — to say this piece works, that one doesn't — a risky enterprise, particularly when no conventional standards, various as those are, apply. I judge according to my lights, which, as Elder Olson says, is all we can ever do; and, as he also says, that severe limitation should not keep us from doing it.

Evaluation has not been the only source of contention among Stein critics, and even now there is no consensus about what she was doing or what is most important in her work. For the sake of perspective, we might survey some of the most important trends in Stein criticism to date. Comparisons of her work to formal techniques of modern painting, particularly cubism, have been important in providing access to the writing, and also in providing an alternative to conventional interpretation.[1] Stein had a deep admiration for Picasso; she emulated him as she emulated no one else. There are significant parallels between her work and his, particularly in the "heroic age of cubism" just before World War I: they share an orientation toward the linguistic or pictorial surface, a movement in and out of recognizable representation; they both shatter or fragment perception and the sentence (or canvas); they both render multiple perspective.[2]

Many writers on Stein have given us a clear picture of her life as art collector, cultural celebrity, influence on the younger generation of writers. The bulk of Stein criticism, in fact, is biographical; her presence, her reputation, is really more that of a "literary figure" than that of a writer. She is seen as someone whose life in literature—her influence, connections, history, witty remarks—is of greater interest and importance than her writing. Some feminist critics are currently interested in Stein's life in literature for very different reasons. Catharine Stimpson, particularly, has shown how Stein encoded a good deal of her "unallowable" lesbian feeling and experience in her radical experimental work.[3]

Discussions of Stein's aesthetic, philosophical, and psychological theories have helped to illuminate the large ideas about time, consciousness, and art which inform her writing.[4] Donald Sutherland's *Gertrude Stein: A Biography of Her Work*,[5] which was the first substantial critical book on Stein's writing and in many ways remains the best (the other work of equal stature is Richard Bridgman's *Gertrude Stein in Pieces*),[6] treats Stein's radical work as illustration of her own version of modernist philosophy and aesthetics.

Many other critics approach Stein's work as illustration, not so much of her own thought, but of that of the philosophers who influenced her: William James and Henri Bergson are the names most commonly invoked; Whitehead, Russell, Santayana, and Hegel also appear.[7] Norman Weinstein updates this approach by connecting Stein to some modern theories of phenomenology and linguistics.[8]

Of recent books on Stein, Richard Bridgman's *Gertrude Stein in Pieces* has been most influential. Its influence is not surprising: his is the first exhaustive, detailed, chronological study of all of Stein's work; he writes with great insight, care, and authority, and his psychobiographical approach is persuasively implemented. Through careful study of Stein's early life and apprentice writing, Bridgman discovers deep insecurity, inertia, passivity, and fear of failure behind her heretofore convincing facade of aggressive confidence in her "genius." He locates the origin of her experimentalism in pathology rather than intention, seeing guilty evasiveness about lesbian sexuality, not concerted innovation, as the crucial origin of the opacity and indeterminacy of her experimental writing. He demonstrates beyond doubt that Stein was tormented by guilt and confusion concerning her sexuality (Catharine Stimpson gives us the cultural origin of this confusion and torment), and that there is a good deal of sexual material in her work which is concealed or encoded in her experimental writing. But by explaining the character of that writing *exclusively* as an evasion of guilty sexual feeling, Bridgman seems to undervalue the conscious, sustained avant-garde radicalism that also propelled Stein's career.[9]

Part of the appeal of Bridgman's approach lies in his discovery of deeper, unconscious motivation beneath conscious authorial intention. Again, this discovery is valid. But perhaps we use our Freudian tools to discount or discredit authorial intention unnecessarily, when we might use them simply to expand our understanding of a particular writer's work and of the creative process in general. A good deal of human activity, and particularly creative activity, is causally overdetermined. We can admit or even focus on Stein's unconscious motivations without using them to replace or discredit her conscious intentions, as Catharine Stimpson shows:

During the decade of choice, Stein both stopped resisting her sexual impulses and found domestic pleasure in them. However, during the same period, if often before the meeting with Toklas, she takes certain lesbian or quasi-lesbian experiences and progressively disguises and encodes them in a series of books. *I would speculate that she does so for several reasons. Some of them are aesthetic:* the need to avoid imitating one's self; the desire to transform apprentice materials into *richer, more satisfying verbal worlds*. Other reasons are psychological: the need to write out hidden impulses; the wish to speak to friends without having others overhear; the desire to evade and to confound strangers, aliens, and enemies.[10] (italics added)

As we see here, a primary interest in recovering her psychological or emotional raw material does not necessarily lead to a hostility toward Stein's experimental style. Stimpson refers to "richer, more satisfying verbal worlds," and Elizabeth Fifer, building on Stimpson's work, speaks of Stein's "startling and meaningfully controlled juxtapositions . . . her use of fascinating 'near meanings'" with which she "proves the worth of her experimental style."[11]

But in a recent book on Stein's portraits, a work of impressive scholarship and careful argument, very helpful on the earlier portraits, Wendy Steiner does call Stein's later, more radical linguistic surface a *"hindrance* to reconstituting the 'meaning' of the words" (italics added).[12] She sees value in the radical writing only in the possibility of retrieving coherent, referential meaning from beneath the linguistic surface:

What I have tried to show is first that the early second-phase portraits are intelligible, second, that they make direct reference to their subjects, and finally, that they call attention to this reference by fairly obvious *clues.* The other important fact about them is that they have an unintelligible surface which, we might say, is *militantly unintelligible* through striking disruptions of syntax, time-space reference, and sense, through the rhyming of words devoid of semantic relation, the multiplication of negatives, and the use of circumlocutions so disjointed as seldom to suggest their *real meaning.*[13] (italics added)

The word "militantly," here clearly pejorative, reveals an essential distrust of the intentional subversiveness of Stein's experimental writing. To benefit by what Stein has to offer, we must accept the "militantly unintelligible" surface without trying to find "real meaning" beneath it.[14]

I might explain how I arrived at my labels for Stein's successive experimental styles. Standard critical terms wouldn't do. I tried for a while to invent my own terms, but ended by appropriating Stein's, mainly from her discussions of her work in *Lectures in America*. Hers, of course, were much better.

A Different Language

CHAPTER 1

Experimental Writing

We might begin by confronting the "difference" of experimental writing:

bins black and green seventh eighth rehearsal pings a bit fussy at times fair scattering grand and exciting world of his fabrication topple out against surface irregularities fragilization of the gut constitutive misrecognitions of the ego most mature artist then in Regina loops of chain into a box several feet away Hiltons and Ritzes fault-tracing forty whacks active enthusiasm old cell is darker and they use the "Don't Know" category less often than younger people I am glad to be here and intend to do what I can to remain mangle stools tables bases and pedestals without my tree. . .(Donald Barthelme, "Bone Bubbles," *City Life*)[1]

 —Well, my positively last at any stage! I hate to look at alarms but, however they put on my watchcraft, must now close as I hereby hear by ear from by seeless socks 'tis time to be up and ambling. Mymiddle toe's mitching, so mizzle I must else 'twill serve me out. Gulp a bulper at parting and the moore the melodest! Farewell but whenever, as Tisdall told Toole. Tempos fidgets. Let flee me fiacckles, says the grand old manoark, stormcrested crowcock and undulant hair, hoodies tway! (James Joyce, *Finnegans Wake*)[2]

Could give no other information than wind walking in a rubbish heap to the sky — Solid shadow turned off the white film of noon heat — Exploded deep in the alley tortured metal Oz — Look anywhere, Dead hand — Phosphorescent bones — Cold Spring afterbirth of that hospital — Twinges of amputation — Bread knife in the heart paid taxi boys — If I knew I'd be glad to look anyplace — No good myself — Clom Fliday — Diseased wind identity fading out — (William Burroughs, *Nova Express*)[3]

Flaunted, leaf-light, drifting at corners, blown across the wheels, silver-splashed, home or not home, gathered, scattered, squandered in separate scales, swept up, down, torn, sunk, assembled — and truth?

Now to recollect by the fireside on the white square of marble. From ivory depths words rising shed their blackness, blossom and penetrate. Fallen the book; in the flame, in the smoke, in the momentary sparks — or now voyaging, the marble square pendant, minarets beneath and the Indian seas, while space rushes blue and stars glint — truth? or now, content with closeness? (Virginia Woolf, "Monday or Tuesday," *A Haunted House and Other Short Stories*)[4]

Light heat white planes shining white one only shining white infinite but that known not. Ping a nature only just almost never one second with image same time a little less blue and white in the wind. Traces blurs light grey eyes holes light blue almost white fixed front ping a meaning only just almost never ping silence. (Samuel Beckett, "Ping," *First Love and Other Shorts*)[5]

In between a place and candy is a narrow foot-path that shows more mounting than anything, so much really that a calling meaning a bolster measured a whole thing with that. A virgin a whole virgin is judged made and so between curves and outlines and real seasons and more out glasses and a perfectly unprecedented arrangement between old ladies and mild colds there is no satin wood shining. (Gertrude Stein, "In Between," *Tender Buttons*)[6]

This writing is hardly uniform. An experimental writer, like any other, has his or her own voice, techniques, imaginative universe. Long literary distances separate Joyce's thickly allusive puns and neologisms, Woolf's flights of quasi-mystical imagery, Burroughs's dead-end "fold-ins," Barthelme's hash of verbal leftovers, Beckett's lean, tight, visionary prose poised over the void, and Stein's comfortable, sensible-seeming, matter-of-fact, wildly unlikely juxtapositions.

But what strikes the reader most forcefully about all of this writing is that it cannot be read in the normal way. Though we can construe sensible meanings here and there with varying degrees of readiness—for Joyce, Woolf, and Beckett we can even find ways, after serious thought, to interpret the whole passage coherently—those constructions can never account more than partially for the writing. These diverse instances of experimental writing are unified, and separated from all conventional writing, by the fact that we cannot interpret any of them to form coherent, single, whole, closed, ordered, finite, sensible meanings, even several such meanings, without radically altering the nature and effect of the writing as it is read.

That obstruction of normal reading is, for the purposes of this study, the most important feature of experimental writing, including Stein's. Gertrude Stein is unique in English, in the sheer quantity and extremity of her experimental writing. Woolf, Beckett, Barthelme, even Burroughs, and certainly Joyce, with the monumental exception of *Finnegans Wake*, do not generally obstruct normal reading as they do above. Stein, throughout her long experimental period, almost always does. But Stein is hardly a dinosaur. Many other writers have written experimentally, many writers are doing so now; writers who find themselves too limited by the modes of expression conventional language provides. Although this book's practical analysis of Stein's experimental styles cannot be applied directly to other experimental writing—since, as is evident above, particular techniques, structures, and configurations of language and meaning vary enormously from writer to writer—its overall sense of experimental writing as an alternative language, which requires a different kind of reading and which opposes itself to the dominant patriarchal culture in definable ways, should apply to all experimental writing.

The unifying feature of experimental writing is, again, the obstruction of normal reading. It prevents us from interpreting the writing to form coherent, single, whole, closed, ordered, finite, sensible meanings. That formulation sounds very much like the vision of all writing postulated by deconstruction. However, there is an important difference. When a deconstructionist such as J. Hillis Miller talks about the "heterogeneity" or the "undecidability" of all literary texts, about their "irresolvable oscillations of meaning," he is not saying that we can never interpret the text coherently, in order to form what Jonathan Culler calls a "thematic synthesis."[7] He means that we can never decide among all the thematic syntheses which it is possible to make of any text. He does not deny that we can generate such syntheses: in fact, he claims that we can generate them *ad infinitum*. What we cannot do is choose from among them any single, "correct reading." With experimental writing, however, we cannot generate thematic syntheses at all. The "irresolvable oscillations of meaning" of deconstruction are sporadic in the non-experimental text; in the experimental text, they are pervasive. In the non-experimental text, posited by deconstruction as "the literary text," incoherence or indeterminacy exists alongside coherence or determinacy, continually challenging, undoing, "deconstructing" it, as the deconstructionist critic does the unitary, coherent interpretations made of that text in the past.

It is interesting, and telling, that deconstructionist critics generally concern themselves with "classic" texts in order to correct our reductive, overly coherent sense of those texts, to reveal them as fluid and amorphous rather than fixed and determinate. But they needn't deconstruct experimental writing, because its indeterminacy and amorphousness, its multiplicity and contradictoriness, are so obvious. Experimental writing has no apparent coherence to deconstruct, no hidden or subtle incoherence to reveal. Hence the difference between the "literary text" of deconstruction and the experimental text as I define it here: the former *can* easily make sense. It is susceptible to thematic synthesis, which the deconstructionist can attack and unravel; the experimental text is not. Even for that experimental writing which comes closest to coherence, and which is partly or marginally susceptible to thematic synthesis (the passages from Woolf, Beckett, Joyce, above), we cannot impose such coherence or synthesis without negating, throwing out, failing to account for, the powerful impression of incoherence the writing initially gives.

In effect, deconstruction is to critical theory what experimental writing is to literature: they posit the same principles and make the same attack. They both posit the principles of literary incoherence or indeterminacy; of "pluridimensionality" or polysemy; they both attack the cultural hegemony of sense, order, linearity, unitary coherence. That hegemony, which generally prevents us from reading and enjoying experimental writing, is manifest in almost all other (non-deconstructive) theoretical discussions of reading and interpretation, whether subjective, affective, positivist, structuralist, psychoanalytic, hermeneutic, or phenomenological.[8]

Simply, we generally reject or repress all meaning in a particular text which does not contribute to some thematic synthesis. In *Structuralist Poetics*,[9] Jonathan Culler seems to epitomize this hegemony by equating the act of (literary) reading itself with interpretation or thematic synthesis.[10] In elaborating his notion of "literary competence," he says that we can read *non*-literary writing simply by understanding the lexical meanings of its words, but in order to read writing "*as* literature," in fact, to understand it at all, we must impose on it some form of thematic synthesis:

> If one knows French, one can translate Mallarmé's 'Salut'. . . but that translation is not a thematic synthesis — it is not what we would ordinarily call 'understanding the poem' — and in order to identify various levels of coherence and set them in relation to one another under the synoptic heading or theme of the 'literary quest' one must have considerable experience of the conventions for reading poetry.[11]

I do not take issue with Culler's important structuralist argument that we bring to a literary text a set of "conventions of reading" which itself creates the text "*as* literature" ("The work has structure and meaning because it is read in a particular way, because these potential properties, latent in the object itself, are actualized by the theory of discourse applied in the act of reading"[12]). The problem comes in the limitation of the "conventions of reading," or "theory of discourse" of "literary reading," to thematic synthesis. There is no room in this formulation for incoherence, for irreducible multiplicity of meaning, or for any form of literary reading that incorporates them, let alone that rejects the "synoptic heading or theme" as its final goal.

At the root of this problem is the equation of the act of reading with the secondary critical process of interpretation or thematic synthesis, an equation which I believe is extremely widespread, and is often at the heart of undergraduate discouragement with the sophistication of professorial "readings" (that use of the word "reading" makes it equivalent to "thematic synthesis"). As George Steiner says, "critic" and "reader" are "not only different but anti-thetical": the reader experiences the text while the critic takes possession of it.[13]

Thematic synthesis is not in fact the immediate result of "competent" reading (Culler defines "literary competence" as knowledge of the conventions of literary discourse). Rather it is the end product of a distinct, complex, and often protracted intellectual process. Culler sees no middle ground, for example, between merely understanding the denotations of the words in Blake's "Ah, Sunflower" and arriving at Harold Bloom's dense, sophisticated thematic synthesis of the poem: "Blake's dialectical thrust at asceticism is more than adroit. You do not surmount Nature by denying its prime claim of sexuality. Instead, you fall utterly into the dull round of its cyclic aspirations."[14] But surely it is possible to imagine reading Blake's poem "competently," beyond rudimentary comprehension of denotation, yet coming nowhere near achieving Bloom's own more than adroit dialectical thrust. And, more important, even Bloom himself must have read the poem many times before he arrived at his final "reading," read with a profound response but one not yet fixed in such an elegantly formulated phrase; a profound response which itself, rather than the end product of critical analysis, should be what we mean by "reading."

Wolfgang Iser would seem to stand alone, among reading theorists, against the hegemony of coherence. He formulates a theory of the *process* of reading which corrects the widespread confusion of reading with the end product of thematic synthesis. However, even though he emphasizes the crucial role of incoherence in the experience of reading literature, he insists on the centrality of constructing coherent patterns of meaning—what he calls "consistency building"—for all literary reading, an insistence which makes impossible a proper reading of intentionally incoherent experimental writing, and therefore denies the alternate literary experience experimental writing offers.

For Iser, incoherence is a necessary but clearly instrumental feature of reading: it exists only in order to allow us to practice our gift for making coherence; for striving, "even if unconsciously, to fit everything together in a consistent pattern."[15] It is precisely the gaps, the moments of inconsistency, indeterminacy, disruption, omission, "blockage of the flow," which *enable* this "consistency building." Iser does allude to the "richness of semantic possibility" available in the "modern text," but he quickly assimilates it as mere "latent disturbance" of coherence. In any text, modern or traditional, the efficacy of interpretation, of discovering thematic coherence, *relies on* the presence of incoherence. Incoherence is important only insofar as it makes the discovery of coherence sufficiently problematic so that the experience of discovery is difficult enough to be genuinely "literary."

The Act of Reading directly engages the issue of deliberate incoherence, or semantic richness in the modern text.[16] But in Iser's discussion of *Ulysses* as a characteristically incoherent modern text, he makes incoherence *the content of* what is actually a thematic synthesis: incoherence itself, the "openness of the world," becomes the unitary theme, the message, the configurative meaning; it is what *Ulysses* is "about." Similarly, *The Sound and the Fury* is *about* "the senselessness of life." In his very denial of the possibility of thematic synthesis of *Ulysses* or *The Sound and the Fury*, Iser produces, precisely, a thematic synthesis, retaining the discovery of A Meaning as the core, the goal, the justification of both reading and criticism.

Iser's grounding in configurative meaning, or thematic synthesis, his use of it as an inevitable point of reference, is an expression of a deep cultural norm, which he seemingly cannot help but affirm, or return to, even when his thinking clearly points in a different direction. It is precisely the norm which intervenes between the reader and the experimental text.

Before we consider how to penetrate that intervention, how to read an experimental text without attempting to impose coherence, we might look at a linguistic model which allows for, validates, and demystifies incoherence: Noam Chomsky's idea of "degrees of grammaticalness."[17] Chomsky establishes three degrees of grammaticalness by differentiating among utterances which are strictly or conventionally grammatical, those which are "semi-grammatical," and those which are totally ungrammatical:

> In short, it seems to me no more justifiable to ignore the distinctions
> of subcategory that give the series "John plays golf," "golf plays John"
> "John plays and," than to ignore the rather similar distinctions
> between seeing a man in the flesh, in an abstract painting, and in an
> inkblot.[18]

Chomsky makes his case for these degrees most convincing simply by giving a list of examples of each degree (I have reversed the order in which he presents them):

> a year ago; perform the task; John plays golf; revolutionary new ideas
> appear infrequently; John loves company; sincerity frightens John;
> what did you do to the book, bite it?

> a grief ago; perform leisure; golf plays John; colorless green ideas
> sleep furiously; misery loves company; John frightens sincerity; what
> did you do to the book, understand it?

> a the ago; perform compel; golf plays aggressive; furiously sleep ideas
> green colorless; abundant loves company; John sincerity frightens;
> what did you do to the book, justice it?[19]

The "semi-grammatical" phrases of the second degree are not sensible, orderly, clear, transparent, immediately graspable, as are the grammatical phrases of the first degree, which corresponds to what I would call conventional writing, whether traditional, modern, or postmodern. Yet these phrases are not devoid of meaning, as are the ungrammatical phrases of the third degree. Some of the semi-grammatical phrases are simply figurative or ironic, highly conventional within literature: "misery loves company," "perform leisure," or "what did you do to the book, understand it?" But the rest of those phrases are typically experimental: "a grief ago," "colorless green ideas sleep furiously," "John frightens sincerity." They are meaningful, readable, suggestive, resonant, with irreducibly multiple connections among their lexical meanings. Both the strangeness and the multiplicity of those linkages make this semi-grammatical, experimental writing "different," alternative, oppositional; the fact that it is *semi-* rather than *un*grammatical is what makes it readable, viable, valid as an option for literature.

The semi-grammatical phrases are strikingly similar to Stein's successful experimental writing, particularly in what I call the "lively words" mode of *Tender Buttons* and the portraits of that period (1911-13). Moreover, unreadable phrases of the third degree such as "a the ago," "perform compel" and "golf plays aggressive" are very similar to the unsuccessful writing that resulted from Stein's interest, in the late twenties and early thirties, in unrelated successions of single words. As Chomsky shows, the difference between the second and third degrees is precisely their accessibility to reading through purposive articulation of meaning; or, as Chomsky puts it, through deviation from, rather than total negation of, conventional grammar.

The second degree of grammaticalness not only undermines or fragments coherent meaning, it also subordinates meaning altogether to the linguistic surface, the signified to the signifier: we notice the strangeness or freshness of the verbal combinations themselves — the words "stand out" *as words* — before we register consciously their dedetermined, unresolved articulations of lexical meanings. And yet, unlike the equally surface-dominated utterances of the third degree of grammaticalness, these deviant utterances retain meaning in some significant, accessible form.

It is important to reiterate the distinction between the intelligibility, or retention of significant, accessible meaning — which I posit for experimental writing — and conventional, referential thematic content (something the writing is "about") — which I believe experimental writing dispenses with almost entirely. As I hope we will see in Stein's writing, the presence of anterior thematic content, a nominal "subject" of a work, is generally irrelevant to the actual nature and effect of experimental writing, and in most cases such a subject is irretrievable without the clue of a title. It seems to me pointless to suppose, for example, that the virtue of *Tender Buttons* is its clarification of our notions of roast beef or asparagus or purses or cushions, or even to suppose that the virtue of Stein's portraits lies in any information they give us about Picasso or Matisse or Mabel Dodge or George Hugnet, as Stein herself clearly tells us:

It really does not make any difference who George Hugnet was or what he did or what I said, all that was necessary was that there was something completely contained within itself and being contained within itself was moving, not moving in relation to anything not moving in relation to itself but just moving, I think I almost at that time did this thing.[20]

Anterior content is for Stein what she generally says it is, here and in her other theoretical writings: irrelevant, an "annoyance," a regrettably necessary focus or "jumping off point" for art:

Most people think that the annoyance that they feel from an oil painting . . . comes from the way the oil painting represents these things, the things represented in the oil painting. But I myself do not think so. I think the annoyance comes from the fact that the oil painting exists by reason of these things the oil painting represents in the oil painting, and profoundly it should not do so, so thinks the oil painting, so sometimes thinks the painter of the oil painting, so instinctively feels the person looking at the oil painting. Really in everybody's heart there is a feeling of annoyance at the inevitable existence of an oil painting in relation to what it has painted people, objects and landscapes.[21]

She reiterates this position firmly and succinctly in "What Are Master-pieces":

In writing about painting I said that a picture exists for and in itself and the painter has to use objects landscapes and people as a way the only way that he is able to get the picture to exist. That is every one's trouble and particularly the trouble just now when every one who writes or paints has gotten to be abnormally conscious of the things he uses that is the events the people the objects and the landscapes and fundamentally the minute one is conscious deeply conscious of these things as a subject the interest in them does not exist.[22]

Accessible meaning is vital to Stein's experimental work, but referential content is not.

We might consider, for example, the following sentence from Stein's "Portrait of Mabel Dodge at the Villa Curonia": "A bottle that has all the time to stand open is not so clearly shown when there is green color there."[23] If we do not treat this writing as nonsense, devoid of meaning, we generally try to *interpret* it: to find in it some coherent, referential content, probably about bottles, ultimately about Mabel Dodge and her milieu at the Villa Curonia. Such efforts at translation generally grant the ambiguity of the writing; for example, that the "green color" might belong either to the bottle itself or to its setting, or that "stand open" might mean either that the bottle is unstoppered or that it is placed in an exposed position. So far the intention and effect of the writing are not violated. However, the translator, asking what Stein's sentence must *really* mean, might then use these alternate readings to generate conventional sentences such as the following, which, taken together, would be offered as both equals and elucidations of Stein's sentence: (1) A bottle meant to be conspicuous does not in fact show up well against a green background. (2) It is not as easy to see or judge the level of liquid in an open bottle when that bottle is green as it is when the bottle is colorless.[24]

The translator might then go on to suppose that Stein was writing about a particular bottle of Mabel Dodge's at the Villa Curonia, either open, half empty, and green, or obscured by an unfortunate green background. This bottle might even be taken as symbolic of "Mabel Dodge at the Villa Curonia"; perhaps Mabel Dodge herself is somehow a "bottle that has all the time to stand open." The possibilities of such symbolic interpretation are just as limitless as they are unconvincing (so unconvincing that one is embarrassed even to mention them).

We can dispense with all of these translations and interpretations, and instead simply register, without any attempt to reconcile, order, extend, apply, or make sense of them, the various meanings the sentence offers. First we are given "a bottle." The reader may or may not at this point visualize a particular bottle. Then we have the modifying phrase "that has all the time to stand open." This phrase offers us essentially two alternate meanings, both equally justifiable: one might see, simultaneously, both a

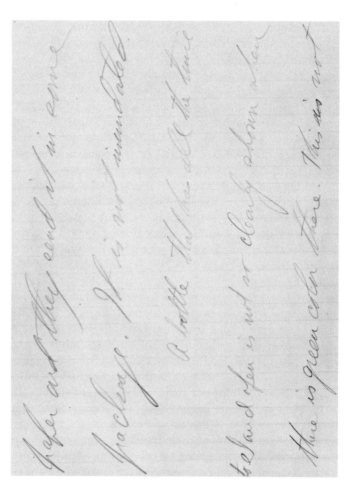

Manuscript page from "Portrait of Mabel Dodge at the Villa Curonia." Courtesy of the Yale Collection of American Literature, Beinecke Rare Book and Manuscript Library, Yale University.

depressingly half-empty forgotten object (covered with dust, neglected, evaporating) and a beautiful, treasured *"objet"* which "has all the time" in the world to "stand open" to the admiration of visitors.

Though these images are contradictory, at least there are only two of them. We would normally expect this ambiguity to be clarified, the sentence to be closed, one possible meaning to be chosen above the other, a meaning which would convey some important information, after the verb "is." But the predicate phrase, "is not so clearly shown when there is green color there," does nothing of the kind. Instead, it multiplies the possible meanings beyond the point where it is even possible to enumerate them. It takes the image we have formed of "a bottle that has all the time to stand open" — an image which the reader may have reduced to one of its possible contours, or which she or he may have allowed to remain in the contradictory doubleness in which the text offers it — and transforms it by forcing it into relation with the idea of being "clearly shown" and then with the idea of "there" being "green color there" ("is" and "when," of course, are what *force* the relation).

Simultaneous thoughts or images flash upon the mind: innumerable instances of the bottle being "not so clearly shown" when "green color" is somehow "there." This reader sees fleeting superimposed images of the depressing, forgotten bottle even more obscured by some sort of green background, by its own green color, by a green spring light, by plants; at the same time the treasured *"objet"* unfortunately obscured by the same multiple forces of greenness. Not only the number of simultaneous images, but their very irreducibility, their unresolvedness, gives rise to a sudden sense of an infinite, limitlessly rich, filled, and open mental, imaginative world, in which we can wander at will without pressure or obstruction: a maze in its complexity, density, and multiplicity of choices, but the opposite of a maze in that there are no wrong turns, no blind alleys, no single correct path, no necessity of forward movement toward exit, no necessity of exit at all.

By choosing the phrases "clearly shown" and "green color" so that they are compatible with "a bottle," Stein allows us to make connections, to form these powerfully rich and undifferentiated configurations of meaning. The writing is capable of being read. But by multiplying ambiguity well beyond what we are used to tolerating even in "difficult" poetry, Stein's sentence absolutely prevents us from making sense. Instead of sense and thematic meaning we have limitless, dense semantic plenitude, and what Roland Barthes calls "*la jouissance de la texte*": writing as erotic celebration, as liberation of meaning from the strictures of hierarchical, sensible, monologistic order.

In *The Pleasure of the Text*, Barthes distinguishes between the text of joy or bliss, which gives the erotic ecstasy of *jouissance*, and the text of mere pleasure.[25] For Barthes, the experimental text — its destruction of order and sense, its simultaneous revelling in the "paradise of words," the anarchic plenitude of language — brings about a flood of joy and freedom so intense that he gives it the erotic name "*jouissance*":

> In short, the word can be erotic on two opposing conditions, both excessive: if it is extravagantly repeated, or on the contrary, if it is unexpected, succulent in its newness (in certain texts, words *glisten*, they are distracting, incongruous apparitions. . .). In both cases,the same physics of bliss, the groove, the inscription, the syncope: what is hollowed out, tamped down, or what explodes, detonates.[26]

Experimental writing is erotic in its excess: the unassimilable excess of meaning, or of repetition, or of sound play, or of surprise. With his "*jouissance de la texte*," his literary "physics of bliss," Barthes formulates dramatically the value to the reader of the alternative experience experimental writing provides.

But the bliss of experimental writing does more than open to us an unfamiliar realm of strangely pleasurable literary experience. That formulation suggests the validation of new experience for its own sake, bringing to mind the insatiable hunger for novel sensation of what we are now calling, after Christopher Lasch, the "culture of narcissism." The *opposition* implicit in experimental writing to the cultural hegemony of sense, order, and coherence has ramifications on the largest scale. Within the framework of longstanding political ideologies, experimental writing expresses or suggests anarchism: the abolition of all forms of hierarchy, of dominance-subordination (in one of her notebooks, Stein said "all great art is anarchy").²⁷ The work of Jacques Derrida and Julia Kristeva allows us to see that experimental writing is also anti-logocentric, hence anti-patriarchal. Experimental writing, by attacking the hegemony of sense, order, and coherence, attacks what Jacques Derrida, in *Of Grammatology*, calls "logocentrism": the arch-conservative principle of all Western culture.²⁸ Logocentrism is many things to Derrida, not all of them relevant to the argument here. But enough of them are relevant to make it worthwhile to construct, briefly, the Derridean mythos of writing yet again. The ascendency, in logocentrism, of speech over writing, and of identity or self-presence over absence, are not important to the development of experimental writing as an alternative language. The crucial component of logocentrism, as far as experimental writing is concerned, has been the ascendency of rationality, linearity, hierarchical order—of the "transcendental signified" of logos—over the play of the signifier. This ascendency makes us think that all language, and particularly all writing, is a mere "secondary representation" of some anterior, absolute meaning or truth (the transcendental signified). As Derrida shows at length, all Western theology and metaphysics, even when seeming to oppose it, endorses the logos, the transcendental signified (God, truth, the principle of principles, etc.).

The configurative meaning or thematic synthesis we expect in literature, the search for which prevents us from reading experimental writing, is one form of the transcendental signified. In logocentrism, the text acquires value and significance only in its revelation of anterior, coherent, referential (transcendent) meaning. Like truth—the logos—statements of theme grant the text value or legitimacy by translating it to a "higher" order of meaning: what was merely a piece of writing becomes a statement about life.

Derridean theory, like experimental writing, reverses this norm. In Derridean deconstruction, the idea of an all-inclusive, unitary configurative meaning is indeed an "illusion": a falsifying construct which covers and distorts the true indeterminacy and plurality of the text. Again, however, the indeterminate, plural text of deconstruction is not the same as the experimental text: it is not radically or thoroughly incoherent, rather it is undecidable. No critical approach can deny the potential for coherent meaning of the conventional text. Deconstruction postulates an irreducible, illimitable multiplicity of separate, often mutually contradictory meanings in the conventional text, each of which may *itself* be coherent. (The distinction I make here between the plural text of deconstruction and the experimental text is precisely Barthes's distinction in "From Work to Text" between the work, which can have "several meanings," and the Text, which has an *"irreducible* plurality" of meaning.)[29] But in deconstruction, the moments of incoherence in the conventional text — the gaps, obstructions, omissions — replace inclusive thematic synthesis as the focus of critical attention. It is this reversal of focus or priority which makes deconstruction essentially sympathetic to experimental writing.

As the characteristic writing of logocentric culture, the conventional text is linear, both in its representation of time and in its (related) structure of successive lines. This structure reflects and endorses the *fiction* of smoothness and coherence on which thematic synthesis, and, more generally, transcendent order and truth, depend. This linearity is not innocent. It has been instituted at the expense of repressing what Derrida calls "pluridimensionality": precisely the irreducible multiplicity we find in experimental writing.

The nonlinear, experimental writing which has reemerged in the modern period is both a challenge to logocentric hegemony and a glimpse or harbinger of a possible cultural order beyond it. Or, to paraphrase Derrida more precisely, nonlinear writing has one face inevitably turned backward toward, or trapped within, the only cultural order we know, but the other face pointing toward the future, in what he calls a "suspense between two ages of writing":[30]

The enigmatic model of the *line* is thus the very thing that philosophy could not see when it had its eyes open on the interior of its own history. This night begins to lighten a little at the moment when linearity — which is not loss or absence but the repression of pluri-

dimensional symbolic thought—relaxes its oppression . . . Not that
the massive reappearance of nonlinear writing interrupts this
structural solidarity; quite the contrary. But it transforms its nature
profoundly. The end of linear writing is indeed the end of the book,
even if, even today, it is within the form of a book that new writings
—literary or theoretical—allow themselves to be, for better or for
worse, encased.[31]

(Like Barthes, Derrida can speak of a "massive reappearance of
nonlinear writing" because French thought generally acknowledges and allies itself with the avant-garde tradition.)

Derrida refers not to the appearance but to the *re*appearance of
nonlinear writing. He postulates a past of nonlinear writing, not
naturally superseded so much as systematically suppressed by
logocentric, linear culture and writing:

We have seen that the traditional concept of time, an entire
organization of the world and of language, was bound up with it (the
linearity of the symbol). Writing . . . is rooted in a past of nonlinear
writing. It had to be defeated, and here one can speak, if one wishes,
of technical success; it assured a greater security and greater
possibilities of capitalization in a dangerous and anguishing world.
But that was not done *one single time*. A war was declared, and a
suppression of all that resisted linearization was installed.[32]

The rationale of this suppression is clear when we make the
crucial linkage of logocentrism with patriarchy, thereby desig-
nating experimental writing as anti-patriarchal. Derrida himself
makes this connection, calling Freudian thought "phallogocentric."[33] Julia Kristeva makes the connection the focus of much of
her work. Along with other feminist theorists and writers such as
Luce Irigaray and Hélène Cixous, Kristeva builds on the work of
Derrida and also of the psychoanalyst Jacques Lacan to arrive at
a profound anti-patriarchal theory of culture and writing.[34]

While Derrida uses "suppression" (political/historical) and "repression" (generally psychological) interchangeably when discussing the forced hegemony of logocentrism over pluridimensionality, through Kristeva (via Lacan) we can incorporate the Freudian
notion of psychic repression into our understanding of that he-

gemony. The notion of psychic repression allows us to posit the equivalence of logocentrism and phallogocentrism, or patriarchy. In spite of the fact that we—both genders—begin to acquire symbolic language well before the resolution of the Oedipal crisis, the conclusive repression of presymbolic language is coincident with the Oedipal phase, which in turn is coincident with full mastery of the use of symbolic language. Symbolic language is simply language as we commonly conceive it: primarily a way to make and order communicable, coherent meaning. It is dominated by the signified. The signifier becomes a more or less transparent communicator of meaning. We are accustomed either to forget or to ignore, except in the restricted areas of learning theory and developmental psychology, the presymbolic state of language we all experience as infants. (Kristeva also calls this language "semiotic," a term I find much less helpful, and more confusing, than the term "presymbolic.") In this presymbolic state, language reaches us as repetition, sound association, intonation: the signifier. What for Derrida is a suppressed cultural/historical past of nonlinear writing can also be seen as a repressed psychological past, in the individual, of presymbolic language. Presymbolic language shares with much experimental writing this ascendency of the signifier: the play of intonation, rhythm, repetition, sound association. Symbolic language is similar to conventional, grammatical, logocentric writing: they both encompass the ascendency of hierarchical order, sense, reason, the signified.

Crucially, we can link the acquisition of symbolic language in the individual with the Freudian acquisition of culture, which takes place at the resolution of the Oedipal crisis by means of capitulation to the dominant, protecting Father-as-cultural-principle. The acquisition of culture, in human society as we know it, *is* the institution of what Jacques Lacan calls the "Rule of the Father," or patriarchy (as anthropologists agree, all existing societies are patriarchal). In Freudian-Lacanian theory, to enter or acquire culture is to embrace simultaneously and exclusively the symbolic order of language and the "Rule of the Father." The two are inseparable, and both come at the cost of repressing, again simultaneously, presymbolic language and the infant's omnipotent, magical unity of the self with the outer world, of which presymbolic language is the expression. The symbolic language of the Father, of patriarchy, is in fact a compensation for that lost omnipotent unity: a means of dominating and controlling the newly alienated outer world.[35] In Lacan's theory, the repression concomitant with acquisition of symbolic language, which he sees as the repression of the ascendent signifier, creates and wholly constitutes the unconscious: the exclusive content of the unconscious is the "autonomous" or "supreme" signifier.[36]

Kristeva and other French feminist theorists of female *"différence"* (as in *"vive la différence"*) extend this formulation, correcting Lacan's (since Freud's) valorization of the phallus. For them, the content of the unconscious, repressed by the institution of the Rule of the Father (patriarchy, phallogocentrism) is what they call the female Other: the pre-Oedipal hegemony of the mother — the *"jouissance* of the mother's body" — which is concomitant with presymbolic language. Irigaray and Cixous, most closely associated with the polemic for female *différence,* argue for the restoration of the repressed female Other, a restoration which would *be,* in Lacan's analysis, the Freudian goal of "making conscious the unconscious." The means for achieving this restoration would be a new women's language, yet to be, or in the process now of being, invented, which develops presymbolic modes of signification.

However, though it is not a specifically female language, written for a female audience, experimental writing is certainly anti-patriarchal according to Kristeva's Lacanian-Derridean construct. To the extent that it relies heavily on aural signification — on the signifier itself — experimental writing is presymbolic, an expression of the pre-Oedipal union with the mother's body, a gesture, against the repression of the Rule of the Father, toward releasing into written culture the power of the Mother. Much or most of Stein's writing is heavily aural, some of it primarily so:

Not so dots large dressed dots, big sizes, less laced, less laced diamonds, diamonds white, diamonds bright, diamonds in the in the light, diamonds light diamonds door diamonds hanging to be four, two four, all before, this bean, lessly, all most, a best, willow, vest, a green guest, guest, go go go go go go, go. Go go. Not guessed. Go go.[37]

Julia Kristeva sees that all features of experimental writing —
pluridimensional, irresolvable multiplicity as well as the dominance of the signifier — are anti-patriarchal:

> For at least a century, the literary avant-garde (from Mallarmé and
> Lautréamont to Joyce and Artaud) has been introducing ruptures,
> blank spaces, and holes into language. . . . All of the modifications in
> the linguistic fabric are the sign of a force that has not been grasped
> by the linguistic or ideological system. This signification renewed,
> "infinitized" by the rhythm in a text, this precisely is (sexual) pleasure
> (*la jouissance*).
>
> However, in a culture where the speaking subjects are conceived of
> as masters of their speech, they have what is called a "phallic"
> position. The fragmentation of language in a text calls into question
> the very posture of this mastery. The writing that we have been
> discussing confronts this phallic position either to traverse it or to
> deny it.[38]

Although its presymbolic foregrounding of the signifier is its only
positive connection to the pre-Oedipal mother, hence to the repressed female Other, experimental writing opposes in every way
the foundations of patriarchal symbolic language. Experimental
writing is only partly explicitly female, of the mother; it is entirely anti-patriarchal. While patriarchal, symbolic language is
sensible, orderly, unitary, dominated by anterior meaning, experimental writing is a "pre-sentence-making disposition to
rhythm, intonation, nonsense; makes nonsense abound within
sense: makes him laugh."[39] Experimental writing "displaces, con-
denses, distributes. It retains all that's repressed by the Word
[patriarchal logos]: by sign, by sense, by communication, by
symbolic order, whatever is legislating, restrictive, paternal."[40]

Experimental writing can liberate, for both genders, the non-
linearity, pluridimensionality, free play of the signifier, the continuity of the order of things with the order of symbols — in sum,
our pre-Oedipal experience of language — an experience which is
repressed by the institutions of patriarchy (phallogocentrism, the
Rule of the Father). But patriarchy is responsible for reason, clarity, and justice as well as impersonality, hierarchy, and tyranny.
Without patriarchal language, this entirely conventional study

of anti-patriarchal language would not be possible. Surely we do not want to liberate the repressed at the expense of destroying the good which repression was instituted to enable. What are the limits of experimental writing?

The first or most obvious limit is of course that it need not replace, or even threaten, conventional writing. Making conscious the unconscious need not destroy the already-conscious; rather, the area of the conscious can be both enlarged and restored to wholeness. One has in mind the kind of balance Kristeva describes in *About Chinese Women,* in her vision of ancient Chinese matrilinear culture. In that culture, neither sexual order had ascendency over the other, neither was repressed or suppressed, and therefore both were equally available, in a "constant alternation between time and its 'truth,' identity and its loss, history and the timeless, signless, extra-phenomenal things that produce it. An impossible dialectic: a permanent alternation: never the one without the other."[41]

This ideal of permanent alternation or dialectic of gender modes, rather than dominance of either, is not merely an afterthought for Kristeva, designed to quell the fears of the male audience. It is central to the project of proposing an alternative to patriarchal language. Indeed, women — as "location" of an alternative to patriarchy — must "refuse all roles, in order, on the contrary, to summon this timeless 'truth' — formless, neither true nor false, echo of our *jouissance,* of our madness, of our pregnancies — into the order of speech and social symbolism."[42] But at the same time we must not "lock ourselves up inside" our female identity after an "initial phase" of "searching for" it;[43] we must "know that an ostensibly masculine, paternal (because supportive of time and symbol) identification is necessary in order to have some voice in the record of politics and history."[44] In this "impossible dialectic" the "paternal identification" (symbolic language, conventional writing) would *coexist* with the "maternal identification" (presymbolic language, experimental writing).[45]

Beyond that crucial but perhaps not obvious qualification, it is also necessary to postulate a related limit *within* experimental writing, a limit implied by the differentiation of "incoherent" from "unintelligible," of "semi-grammatical" from "ungrammati-

cal." Simply, successful experimental writing generally requires
the presence of articulated meaning in the text. Again, to repudiate coherent meaning is not to repudiate meaning altogether.
Meaning can be present and available in the text in multiple, undetermined, fragmented form. But without some concerted articulation of meaning, most experimental texts are unreadable.[46]

The apparent contradiction in experimental writing between
its destruction of sense and its retention of a "paternal identification" (what Barthes calls, in *The Pleasure of the Text*, the "shadow
of the text" of bliss) — the felt presence of articulated meaning —
parallels a contradiction in Stein's own esthetic theory. In her lectures and essays, Stein elaborates two central, contradictory
threads of argument: literature must be absolutely pure (serve
"god" rather than "mammon," in Stein's terminology), but at the
same time it must express and create its time, its "composition."[47]
It must both renounce the world and embody the deepest nature,
the essence, of its cultural moment.

In her extensive elaboration of the notion of artistic autonomy
or purity, it is clear that Stein considers communicated content
irrelevant to value in art. Artistic merit is exclusively a matter of
imagination and perfection of form within a particular medium.
Great literature is recognizable by qualities independent of its
content: by "its complete solidity, its complete imagination, its
complete existence."[48] The subject of a masterpiece might be
steeped in contingency, but the work itself must be free of it:

After all any woman in any village or men either if you like or even
children know as much of human psychology as any writer that ever
lived. After all there are things you do know each one in his or her
way knows all of them and it is not this knowledge that makes
master-pieces. . . . Those who recognize master-pieces say that is the
reason but it is not. It is not the way Hamlet reacts to his father's
ghost that makes the master-piece, he might have reacted according to
Shakespeare in a dozen other ways and everybody would have been
as much impressed by the psychology of it. . . . master-pieces . . .
exist because they came to be as something that is an end in itself and
in that respect it is opposed to the business of living which is relation
and necessity. That is what a master-piece is not although it may
easily be what a master-piece talks about. ("What Are Master-pieces,"
149, 151)

However, this pure work of art is, paradoxically, both characteristic and constitutive of its time; for Stein, the "modern composition":

> People really do not change from one generation to another, . . .
> nothing changes from one generation to another except the things seen
> and the things seen make that generation, that is to say nothing
> changes in people from one generation to another except the way of
> seeing and being seen, the streets change, the way of being driven in
> the streets change, the buildings change, the comforts in the houses
> change, but the people from one generation to another do not change.
> The creator in the arts is like all the rest of the people living, he is
> sensitive to the changes in the way of living and his art is inevitably
> influenced by the way each generation is living, . . . Really the
> composition of this war, 1914–1918, was not the composition of all
> previous wars, the composition was not a composition in which there
> was one man in the centre surrounded by a lot of other men but a
> composition that had neither a beginning nor an end, a composition
> of which one corner was as important as another corner, in fact the
> composition of cubism. (*Picasso*, 10–11)

> One must never forget that the reality of the twentieth century is not
> the reality of the nineteenth century, not at all and Picasso was the
> only one in painting who felt it, the only one. More and more the
> struggle to express it intensified. Matisse and all the others saw the
> twentieth century with their eyes but they saw the reality of the
> nineteenth century, Picasso was the only one in painting who saw the
> twentieth century with his eyes and saw its reality and consequently
> his struggle was terrifying, terrifying for himself and for the others,
> because he had nothing to help him, the past did not help him, nor
> the present, he had to do it all alone . . .(*Picasso*, 21–22)

Stein's reiteration of "the only one *in painting*" implies that she is thinking of her own terrifying, solitary struggle. But what is the nature of that struggle? To realize the modern composition, as she indicates here, or to free her work from all forms of contingency?

Stein's thought offers no synthesis, no answer to that question. Her unwitting theoretical alternation between the norms of artistic purity and of expressing/creating the modern composition in fact resembles the ideal cultural alternation, the permanent dialectic, which Kristeva proposes between the modes of the Mother and the Father. It is not necessary, therefore, to try to resolve this contradiction at the theoretical level, as long as it is resolved in practice: as long as Stein's writing is incoherent rather than unintelligible, semi-grammatical rather than ungrammatical; as long as she articulates lexical meanings in a way that allows us to read.

CHAPTER 2

Three Lives

Gertrude Stein had written the story of Melanctha. . .which was the first definite step away from the nineteenth century and into the twentieth century in literature. (The Autobiography of Alice B. Toklas, 54)

S tein composed *Three Lives* while she stared at Cézanne's portrait of his wife and while she sat for Picasso's portrait of herself. It represents her first concerted break with conventional modes of writing. It is crucial to her experimental career, both as the source of her subsequent stylistic techniques and as a clue to the source of her rebellion against patriarchal linguistic structures.

Stein's break with literary convention in *Three Lives* is generally described as stylization of the prose surface in order to render directly the essence of a character's identity, which Stein calls the pulse of personality, and the critic Norman Weinstein calls the unique "rhythm, density, continuity, speed, quantity" of consciousness.[1] Stein also manipulates the prose surface in *Three Lives* in order to render directly what she calls a "continuous present": a notion of time, derived from William James and akin to that of Henri Bergson, as a continuous process or succession of steadily shifting present moments rather than a linear progress or march from past through present to future. This stylization of the prose surface is seen by many critics as the beginning of

Stein's progress toward an abstract, self-contained, plastic, autonomous literature, whose only concern is its articulation of formal features of language. As Richard Bridgman says, " While such examples [of dialogue from *Melanctha*] are still tied to the story, it is not difficult to see how they could easily lead to a preoccupation with the prose surface itself, at the expense of the imagined reality she was attempting to create."[2] Michael Hoffman makes a similar, even clearer statement:

How does Stein move within just a few years from a stylized Jamesian realism to both a fragmented narrative structure and a ritualized style, and then, within less than a decade, turn to a use of language in which words cease to be purveyors of conventional meaning and become plastic counters to be manipulated purely in obedience to the artist's expressive will, just as painters manipulate nonsemantic line and color?[3]

Such judgments proceed from a concept of literary meaning borrowed from painting, where meaning must be either referential or abstract. Meaning in experimental writing need be neither: it often has no anterior, referential, thematic content, yet it has readable meaning — it is not abstract. Bridgman is certainly correct that Stein begins, with *Melanctha*, to abandon "the imagined reality she was attempting to create." But the "preoccupation with the prose surface" which leads her to do so is not, as Hoffman has it, a retreat from meaning into pure form. Rather it is the beginning of a shift from conventional, patriarchal to experimental, anti-patriarchal modes of articulating meaning.

The origins of this shift are clearest in the *overt* stylistic innovations of *Melanctha*, but they are also embedded in some of the more familiar modernist or impressionist features of all three novellas. Like a good deal of early modern fiction, *Three Lives* employs the device of obtuse or unreliable narration.[4] Generally, obtuse narration is a function of subjectivity: the narrator's psychology and involvement in the story determine her or his version of it. By allowing for this subjective structuring, we are able simultaneously to chart the limits of the narrator's perception and to see beyond them (this process is often facilitated by multiple narration, as in Conrad's *Nostromo*, Woolf's *To The Light-house*, etc.). In *Three Lives*, the narration is "omniscient third," yet nonetheless obtuse: there is a discrepancy, sometimes to the point of contradiction, between the tone of the narrative voice and the content of the narrative. Some such discrepancy is, as we know, characteristic of fiction, where irony, understatement, or a conflict of conscious and unconscious creation so often generates a complex vision. But in *Three Lives*, the discrepancy is so extreme that the narrator seems at times entirely blind to the import of what she narrates.

While the narrative voice of *Three Lives* is consistently innocent, straightforward, mildly jolly, and approving, the content is often grotesque, sinister, ridiculous. The gulf between what the narrator tells us and what we see is most vivid in some of the brilliant brief portraits, such as this one of Mrs. Haydon, Lena's aunt:

> This aunt, who had brought Lena, four years before, to Bridgepoint, was a hard, ambitious, well meaning, german woman. . . . Mrs. Haydon was a short, stout, hard built, german woman. She always hit the ground very firmly and compactly as she walked. Mrs. Haydon was all a compact and well hardened mass, even to her face, reddish and darkened from its early blonde, with its hearty, shiny cheeks, and doubled chin well covered over with the uproll from her short, square neck.[5]

The avuncular simplicity, the cheerful straightforwardness of the narrator's tone, the words "well meaning" and "hearty," muffle the frightening, repulsive discord of the "hardened mass" and the "doubled chin well covered over with the uproll from her short, square neck." If we visualize Mrs. Haydon from this description, we see a monster, which is precisely what she becomes in the course of the story.

One of the best brief portraits is of Anna's half brother, the baker:

> Her half brother, the fat baker, was a queer kind of a man. He was a huge, unwieldy creature, all puffed out all over, and no longer able to walk much, with his enormous body and the big, swollen, bursted

veins in his great legs. He did not try to walk much now. He sat around his place, leaning on his great thick stick, and watching his workmen at their work.

On holidays, and sometimes of a Sunday, he went out in his bakery wagon. He went then to each customer he had and gave them each a large, sweet, raisined loaf of caky bread. At every house with many groans and gasps he would descend his heavy weight out of the wagon, his good featured, black haired, flat, good natured face shining with oily perspiration, with pride in labor and with generous kindness. Up each stoop he hobbled with the help of his big stick, and into the nearest chair in the kitchen or in the parlour, as the fashion of the house demanded, and there he sat and puffed, and then presented to the mistress or the cook the raisined german loaf his boy supplied him. (*Three Lives*, 48)

The incongruity in this portrait of the baker is summarized in the "good featured, black haired, flat, good natured face shining with oily perspiration, with pride in labor and with generous kindness." The negative "oily perspiration" is included casually, as if it conveyed the same message as the more positive "good features," "good nature," "pride in labor," and "generous kindness."

The narrative voice in *Three Lives* is not only straightforward, factual, reassuring; it is also childish, whimsical, consciously naive: the baker is "a queer kind of a man," "all puffed out all over," who "sits and puffs" in the kitchens of his customers. The diction and tone could be those of a children's story. This childish language heightens the discrepancy between narrative voice and content, here and elsewhere by means of its implied innocence concerning what seems a sexually charged disgust, and more generally in the novellas by masking the sophisticated complexity and somber implications of Stein's "imagined reality."

The three women's lives of the title all end in defeated, lonely death, a fact one would never surmise from the narrative tone. Anna, a generous, hardworking, stubborn, managing German immigrant (based on one of Stein's Baltimore servants), works herself to death for a series of selfish employers and friends who take all she offers, allow her to run their lives (the only repayment she exacts), then desert her when she has outlived her usefulness or when they are tired of her rigid control. She dies poor, of an unnamed disease, alone except for the one friend (Mrs. Drehten, the long-suffering, passive victim of poverty and a tyrannical husband) whose society represents no hope whatever of improving Anna's lot.

As "the good Anna" dies of her goodness, "the gentle Lena" dies of her gentleness. She is passive, dreamy, absent, slow-witted, but of touch with her feelings. She is forced into marriage by her aunt, the monstrous ("well meaning," "hearty") Mrs. Haydon, with the equally passive yet reluctant Herman Kreder. Herman comes into his own by triumphing over his fairytale witch of a mother — something his marriage has given him the strength to do — and his children give purpose and vitality to his life. Lena, unable to assert or even to know her will, steadily fades into near nonexistence, and dies giving birth to the fourth child.

Melanctha, who has no summarizing fatal female virtue, has a more complex death than Anna or Lena. Melanctha's story had been told before by Stein, in her first novel, originally entitled Q.E.D. (1903–5).[6] Q.E.D. is a straightforward account of Stein's first lesbian affair with May Bookstaver, whom she met while at Johns Hopkins Medical School. May was attached to a third woman whom she would not give up. The affair ended, in stalemate, with Stein's expatriation to Paris.[7] The triangle, origin of the title Q.E.D., is absent in Melanctha, which focuses on the temperamental differences between Jeff Campbell, Stein's surrogate, and Melanctha, a transformation of May. Jeff's involvement with Melanctha — his painful growth and final disappointment — is the center of the story, but only one episode in Melanctha's life. Melanctha, an intelligent, reckless black woman, is a much more complicated heroine/victim than Anna or Lena (Stein calls her the "complex desiring Melanctha"). Where Anna is defeated simply by her goodness and Lena by her gentleness, Melanctha is defeated by what is emerging as the fatal flaw par excellence of heroines in women's fiction: a divided self.[8] At crucial times in her life, including the moment when she finally has the full and passionate love she needs from Jeff, she acts against her own best interests, destroying the relationships she has worked hard to build. "Melanctha Herbert was always seeking rest and quiet, and always she could only find new ways to be in trouble" (89).

From Jeff she moves on to Jem Richards, an unreliable gambler, and to the shallow, selfish Rose Johnson. She loses Jem by pressing him when he's down, and finally she loses her last hope for safety, Rose Johnson, by being too kind to Rose's husband Sam. She dies of consumption, alone, in a sanatorium for the poor. These plot summaries are accurate and yet misleading. The bitter implications, the powerful feminist morals of these stories (the "good" woman who dies of service to others, the "gentle" woman who dies in unwanted childbirth, the "complex, desiring" woman who dies of self-defeating complexity and unsatisfied desire) are concealed or overruled not only by the narrator's tone and diction but also by narrative emphasis and temporal structure. While Stein's uses of obtuse narration to distance language ironically from content and to avoid forcing on the reader any judgment of the story seem intentional (she was translating Flaubert's *Un Coeur Simple* when she began *Three Lives*), her use of narrative tone and temporal structure as a defense against her own anger and despair appears unconscious. Throughout the novellas, Stein seems primarily interested in the comic manifestations of her heroines' psychologies, or in the inverse relation, among friends and lovers, between power and need, or in clashes resulting from the attraction of opposite temperaments. One has no sense that Stein recognizes what is clear in each plot: the defeat of a woman by dominant personality traits which are culturally defined as female. The three deaths of this trilogy are achieved in quick closing sections, almost appended as afterthought or postscript (only *The Good Anna* is divided into parts; "Part III, The Death of the Good Anna" takes up six of the story's seventy-one pages; Melanctha dies in half a page, Lena in half a paragraph).

Our attention is also diverted from the thematic implications of the plots by the characteristically impressionist temporal structure of *Three Lives*. Impressionist narrative generally begins on the eve of an important event or time, without letting the reader know that it has any particular significance. The story then "flashes back" to the events or times in the protagonist's life which build to this crucial moment, constructing the whole picture through an accretion of episodes, until the reader has a full sense of the import of that initial moment. Both *The Good Anna* and *The Gentle Lena* begin during the short time of the heroine's happiness (in service to a congenial mistress) which just precedes the reversal of her fortunes; the greater part of each story is a flashback to the life that led to that pinnacle. *Melanctha* begins with the death of Rose Johnson's baby, an episode which, despite its casual cruelty, seems at first to have no negative implications for Melanctha. Since we do not know that these initial moments immediately precede the heroine's defeated death, each novella seems to be progressing not toward death but toward a happy, or at least promising time in the character's life. (Stein in fact holds out false hope for Melanctha in the beginning of her story: "Melanctha Herbert had not *yet* been really married" [85; italics added].) It is this structure which gives the deaths of the heroines the quality of afterthought or postscript, distracting us from their actual thematic centrality.

Temporal structure works against thematic structure on other levels within *Three Lives*. The morals of these three tales depend on linear causality: Anna can be said to die of her goodness only insofar as we can see her becoming worn out and sick *because* she works too hard, eats too little, gives all her money to her friends. But linear causality in *Three Lives* is counteracted or counterbalanced by two conflicting temporal models, one which Stein calls the "continuous present," and the other which we might call "spatial form," or simply stasis.[9] To the extent that the time of the narrative is a "continuous present," the chronological events in each heroine's life are not linked causally. Instead, they are seen as a process of continual change, where one condition or state of being persists for a time and then is either suddenly transformed or gradually shifted into a different (often opposite) condition. But whether change is sudden or gradual, it is part of the natural process of life and not dependent on the will of a character or the logic of other events in the narrative. Change is often sudden: "And so Jeff Campbell went on with this dull and sodden, heavy, quiet always in him, and he never seemed to be able to have any feeling. Only sometimes he shivered hot with shame when he remembered some things he once had been feeling. And then one day it all woke up, and was sharp in him" (*Melanctha*, 194).

For gradual change, which is most characteristic of the "continuous present," Stein uses the word "now":

> Jeff Campbell never asked Melanctha any more if she loved him. Now things were always getting worse between them. Now Jeff was always very silent with Melanctha. Now Jeff never wanted to be honest to her, and now Jeff never had much to say to her.
>
> Now when they were together, it was Melanctha always did most of the talking. Now she often had other girls there with her. . . .
>
> Every day it was getting harder for Jeff Campbell. It was as if now, when he had learned to really love Melanctha, she did not need any more to have him. Jeff began to know this very well inside him. . . .
>
> Every day Melanctha Herbert was less and less near to him. She always was very pleasant in her talk and to be with him, but somehow now it never was any comfort to him.
>
> Melanctha Herbert now always had a lot of friends around her. Jeff Campbell never wanted to be with them. Now Melanctha began to find it, she said it often to him, always harder to arrange to be alone now with him. (*Melanctha*, 188–189)

With each "now," the situation is slightly worse. Stein captures a process which takes place over a period of time without isolating a past time from the "continuous present" of the narrative.

Though the kinetic model of time (life as constant change) dominates the narrative structure, the static, anti-developmental temporal model is reflected in the circularity (minus death) of each novella, as well as in the internal structure of many vignettes. Lena sits in the park with the other servant girls, her friends, who always tease her. One day she is playing with a green paper accordion that her young charge has dropped. One of her friends, Mary, suddenly asks her what she has on her finger.

> "Why, what is it, Mary, paint?" said Lena, putting her finger to her mouth to taste the dirt spot.
>
> "That's awful poison Lena, don't you know?" said Mary, "that green paint that you just tasted."
>
> Lena had sucked a good deal of the green paint from her finger. She stopped and looked hard at the finger. She did not know just how much Mary meant by what she said.
>
> "Ain't it poison, Nellie, that green paint, that Lena sucked just

now," said Mary. "Sure it is Lena, its real poison, I ain't foolin' this time anyhow."

Lena was a little troubled. She looked hard at her finger where the paint was, and she wondered if she had really sucked it.

It was still a little wet on the edges and she rubbed it off a long time on the inside of her dress, and in between she wondered and looked at the finger and thought, was it really poison that she had just tasted.

"Ain't it too bad, Nellie, Lena should have sucked that," Mary said. . . .

And so they all three sat with their little charges in the pleasant sunshine a long time. And Lena would often look at her finger and wonder if it was really poison that she had just tasted and then she would rub her finger on her dress a little harder. (*The Gentle Lena*, 241–42)

There is no climax, no denouement: just a simple, static event, with all the participants acting in characteristic ways. Crucially, development is replaced by repetition, as each character reveals her essence by repeating the actions (Mary's teasing, Lena's dumb, comic sucking, staring, and worrying) which Stein uses to identify or symbolize it.

As in much impressionist and modernist fiction, narrative tone and temporal structure are at odds in *Three Lives* with the thematic content deducible from close reading and a reconstruction of linear causality. The tone and emphasis are noncommittal, cheerful, naive, at most mildly mocking; the thematic content is bitter, angry, implying a sophisticated social-political awareness and judgment. Temporal structure is preponderantly either a "continuous present" or static, yet each novella plots a classic trajectory of rise and fall. Nothing better epitomizes the contradictions of *Three Lives* than its epigraph, a quotation from Jules Laforgue: "Donc je suis un malheureux et ce/n'est ni ma faute ni celle de la vie." These lines certainly belie the narrator's cheerful innocence, but they equally belie the conclusions we can draw with excellent justification from all three novellas that a cruel "life," at least, is very much to blame for the mistreatment and death of these women.

We need no longer speculate about the psychological reasons

for Stein's diverting attention, both her own and the reader's, from her anger and sadness. Richard Bridgman and Catharine Stimpson have shown with great clarity that Stein simultaneously concealed and encoded in her literary work troublesome feelings about herself as a woman, about women's helplessness, and particularly about lesbianism, still very much considered by society a "pollutant," as Stimpson puts it, during most of Stein's life.[10] But Stein did not merely stifle or deny her anger, her sense that she did not fit and that the deficiency was not hers but rather that of the structure which excluded her. In effect, Stein's rebellion was channelled from content to linguistic structure itself.[11] A rebellion in language is much easier to ignore or misconstrue, but its attack, particularly in literature, penetrates far deeper, to the very structures which determine, within a particular culture, what can be thought.

Stein's anti-patriarchal rebellion was not conscious or intentional, as her denial of her own bitterness and anger in *Three Lives* suggests. But for her, as perhaps for Virginia Woolf, there is an extra dimension to the view of experimental writing as anti-patriarchal, because both writers defined themselves in opposition to the notions of women which patriarchy provides.

Stein's attitude toward her gender offers further material for speculation. As we will see in greater detail in Chapter 7, when this material becomes particularly relevant to Stein's writing, her female self-hatred was such that she was psychologically compelled to identify herself as a man in order to be a happy, sexually active person and a functioning writer. While she lived with her brother Leo, she was a frequently depressed, subservient sister; when Leo left and Alice Toklas moved in, she became a generally happy, very productive husband. This male identification did not shift until the late twenties, when there is evidence that Stein began to feel better about her female identity. Throughout her radically experimental period, therefore, she essentially thought of herself as a man (there is direct evidence of this identification in the notebooks, where Stein says "Pablo & Matisse have a maleness that belongs to genius. Moi aussi, perhaps").[12] We might posit a speculative connection between this male identification, and the concomitant suppression of her female identity, with the shift of the rebellious impulse from thematic content to linguistic structure, where the subversive implications of the writing are at once more powerful and more abstruse.

In relying totally on language itself to effect the transformation of the world, Stein is also very squarely within what Richard Poirier has identified as the American literary tradition in which rebellious imaginers use style to create an alternative "world elsewhere." Writers in this tradition

resist within their pages the forces of environment that otherwise dominate the world. Their styles have an eccentricity of defiance . . . they [try] to create an environment of "freedom," though as writers their efforts must be wholly in language. American books are often written as if historical forces cannot possibly provide such an environment, as if history can give no life to "freedom," and as if only language can create the liberated place.[13]

Within *Three Lives*, narrative tone and temporal structure serve to detach the text from its (at least formally) more traditional elements of thematic content and causative sequence, but to no significantly greater extent than do the impressionist structures and obtuse or multiple narrations of many other early modern novels.[14] However, impressionist structure and obtuse narration have a different significance in this early work of Stein's than they have for Conrad or even Faulkner. For Stein, the detachment of writing from coherent thematic content is the beginning of leaving such content behind altogether, of attempting to create "the liberated place" entirely through language. In *Three Lives*, in addition to these impressionist forms, we begin to see some of the experimental stylistic techniques Stein will use to develop antipatriarchal modes of literary signification, independent of coherent, referential, unitary meaning, hierarchical order, and the dominant signified.

Much has been made of the way Stein uses voice in *Three Lives* to abstract the essence of personality or consciousness of each character — what Donald Sutherland calls "the extremely delicate sequence and emphasis of the ideas as they come out of the character in accordance with the vital intensity and frequency of that character,"[15] and Norman Weinstein labels the character's "density, continuity, speed and quantity" of consciousness. Stein simply calls it the rhythm or pulse of personality, which she tries to re-create in language.

One might question whether this re-creation is essentially different from the handling of speech in other writing. Certainly, great writers of all periods, and in all genres and styles — from Shakespeare through Dickens and Browning to Joyce and Faulkner — have found ways to differentiate and animate their characters' voices. However, there is a difference between achieving a vivid, full, unique characterization through voice, and translating the abstract essence of a character's consciousness into patterns of language. Whereas Dickens uses voice to reveal a character's eccentricity, or Joyce pours out the contents of a character's consciousness in an appropriate flood of words, Stein establishes an equivalence between abstract qualities of consciousness and formal qualities of language: a particular "pulse" ("density, continuity, speed, quantity") of consciousness becomes a particular kind of syntax, phrasing, rhythm, diction, tone. Character is translated into, rather than revealed by, speech. As in all artistic stylization, this translation creates (or reveals) a distance between the work of art and its subject or referential content; a distance which it is the purpose of realistic art (art of verisimilitude) to deny or conceal. For Stein, this distance is another origin of the full separation of writing from coherent thematic content which characterizes her later work.

The stylization in Stein's voice-portraiture — her transformation of psychological essences into patterns of speech — appears from the outset in *Three Lives*, in *The Good Anna*. The difference in diction, phrasing, rhythm and syntax between Anna's tense, direct, abrupt, staccato voice and Mrs. Lehntman's soft, vague, diffuse, conciliatory voice has frequently been noted.

As always with Anna when a thing had to come it came very short and sharp. She found it hard to breathe just now, and every word came with a jerk.

"Mrs. Lehntman, it ain't true what Julia said about your taking that Lily's boy to keep. I told Julia when she told me she was crazy to talk so."

Anna's real excitements stopped her breath, and made her words come sharp and with a jerk. Mrs. Lehntman's feelings spread her breath, and made her words come slow, but more pleasant and more easy even than before.

"Why Anna," she began, "don't you see Lily couldn't keep her boy for she is working at the Bishops' now, and he is such a cute dear little chap, and you know how fond I am of little fellers, and I thought it would be nice for Julia and for Willie to have a little brother." (*The Good Anna*, 43)

The simplicity of language in this passage masks the complexity of its construction: Stein controls prose style very carefully to render the pulse of each personality.

The prose of *The Good Anna* and *The Gentle Lena* is still well within the bounds of conventionality. However, it is more rhythmic and poetic than most conventional prose, with an unusual frequency of iambic sequences, alliteration and internal rhyme: "But they could mourn together for the world these two worn, working german women, for its sadness and its wicked ways of doing. Mrs. Drehten knew so well what one could suffer" (*The Good Anna*, 69). The rhythmic quality of the prose is linked, as we shall see more clearly in *Melanctha*, to its repetitiveness:

Lena was a brown and pleasant creature, brown as blonde races often have them brown, brown, not with the yellow or the red or the chocolate brown of sun burned countries, but brown with the clear color laid flat on the light toned skin beneath, the plain, spare brown that makes it right to have been made with hazel eyes, and not too abundant straight, brown hair, hair that only later deepens itself into brown from the straw yellow of a german childhood. (*The Gentle Lena*, 240)

With so much repetition, and with a vocabulary so carefully limited to simple, commonplace words, Stein achieves surprisingly compact and nuanced description in this early prose, particularly in her protraiture:

Herman Kreder did not care much to get married. He was a gentle soul and a little fearful. He had a sullen temper, too. He was obedient to his father and his mother. He always did his work well. He often

went out on Saturday nights and on Sundays, with other men. He
liked it with them but he never became really joyous. He liked to be
with men and he hated to have women with them. He was obedient
to his mother, but he did not care much to get married. (*The Gentle
Lena*, 251)

Diction and word order are already somewhat unconventional
in *The Good Anna* and *The Gentle Lena*, giving the prose a quality of strangeness and surprise:

She would call and wait a long time and then call again, always even,
gentle, patient, while the young ones fell back often into that
precious, tense, last bit of sleeping that gives a strength of joyous
vigor in the young, over them that have come to the readiness of
middle age, in their awakening. (*The Gentle Lena*, 239)

Finally, Stein repeats key phrases throughout *The Good Anna*
and *The Gentle Lena* which, like operatic motifs, both identify
and represent her characters: "Mrs. Lehntman was the one romance in Anna's life," "Anna led an arduous and troubled life,"
"Lena was patient, gentle, sweet and german."
   The iambic rhythms and other poetic devices call attention to
the prose in a conventional way, and are not particularly important for Stein's later experimental writing. However, the limitation of vocabulary, the condensation, the repetition, the surprising diction and the unconventional word order are crucial
discoveries for Stein. They are points of departure, from which
many characteristic features of her experimental styles evolve.
   The most noticeable feature of Stein's writing between 1906
and 1911 is its repetitiveness. It is undoubtedly safe to assert that
no other writer has ever used repetition as extensively as Stein
did in this period. In his book *Telling It Again and Again*, Bruce
Kawin sees repetition, including Stein's, as isolating and in effect
bracketing the unadulterated present moment, and therefore
coming as close as writing can to a positive version of "silence" (a
mystical, super-verbal, transcendent, absolute truth).[16] Stein herself considered repetition the truth about time, consciousness,
personality, knowing; for her it needed no further justification.

Other analyses of literary repetition emphasize, as I will, its incantatory, hypnotic effect on the reader.[17]

Repetition is a complex, overdetermined phenomenon in *Three Lives*. Partly, its purpose is mimetic: it gives a truer representation than standard writing of the raw process of consciousness. Characters and narrator in *Three Lives* all speak as their minds work, expressing the sequence of their contradictory, ambivalent thoughts and feelings, coming to no conclusions, using language both to reveal the process of consciousness and to grope toward a connection with its inchoate contents. Like a fixated, blocked mind struggling to free itself by going over and over the terms of its fixation until it has mastered them, Stein's narrator ruminates over Jeff's feelings and the dynamic of his relationship with Melanctha, pushing the story slowly forward, gradually achieving a full statement of her vision. Jeff makes a parallel struggle toward understanding himself and mastering the terms of his fixation on Melanctha. Each time the narrator rethinks the situation, she both re-covers the same ground and adds a little new territory, so that the picture slowly becomes both larger and clearer. Jeff struggles to understand, and the narrator struggles to understand Jeff's struggle:

Then it came that Jeff knew he could not say out any more, what it was he wanted, he could not say out any more, what it was, he wanted to know about, what Melanctha wanted. . . . And slowly now, Jeff soon always came to be feeling that his Melanctha would be hurt very much in her head in the ways he never liked to think of, if she would ever now again have to listen to his trouble, when he was telling about what it was he still was wanting to make things for himself really understanding.

Now Jeff began to have always a strong feeling that Melanctha could no longer stand it, with all her bad suffering, to let him fight out with himself what was right for him to be doing. . . . He never could be honest now, he never could be now, any more, trying to be really understanding, for always every moment now he felt it to be a strong thing in him, how very much it was Melanctha Herbert always suffered. . . .

Jeff did not like it very well these days, in his true feeling. He knew now very well Melanctha was not strong enough inside her to stand any more of his slow way of doing. And yet now he knew he was not honest in his feeling. Now he always had to show more to Melanctha than he was ever feeling. Now she made him go so fast, and he knew it was not real with his feeling, and yet he could not make her suffer so any more because he always was so slow with his feeling.

It was very hard for Jeff Campbell to make all this way of doing, right, inside him. If Jeff Campbell could not be straight out, and real honest, he never could be very strong inside him. . . .

Jeff Campbell never knew very well these days what it was that was going on inside him. All he knew was, he was uneasy now always to be with Melanctha . . . not the way he used to be from just not being very understanding, but . . . because he knew now he was having a straight good feeling with her, but she went so fast, and he was so slow to her; Jeff knew his right feeling never got a chance to show itself as strong, to her.

All this was always getting harder for Jeff Campbell. He was very proud to hold himself to be strong, . . . He was very tender not to hurt Melanctha, ... he hated that he could not now be honest with her, he wanted to stay away to work it out all alone, without her, he was afraid she would feel it to suffer, if he kept away now from her. He was uneasy always, with her, . . . he knew now he had a good, straight, strong feeling of right loving for her, and yet now he never could use it to be good and honest with her. (Melanctha, 161–164)

It would be almost impossible to paraphrase this passage, comprised as it is of continually shifting shades of meaning. Although we can scarcely pinpoint the moment when a new idea or new information is introduced, we feel by the end of the passage that we know much more than we did at the beginning. We feel as if we are living through an experience rather than reading about it; we come away with a feeling of deep familiarity with or rootedness in the dimensions of the situation unextended to a coherent intellectual grasp of them. Melanctha is a significant step away from writing which invites thematic synthesis.

The repetition so noticeable in this writing is closely related to the other innovative stylistic features of Melanctha that were so fruitful for Stein's later work: the present participles, gerunds, progressive verb forms — "-ing words" for convenience's sake — the incantatory rhythm, the rhyming, the superfluous words and punctuation, the abstract vocabulary and the emblematic use of certain key words. The compact, evenly stressed rhythms of The

Good Anna and *The Gentle Lena* are transformed by repetition in *Melanctha* into a wavelike cadence with phrases or measures emphasized by rhymes. Contrast these two passages, the first from *The Good Anna* and the second from *Melanctha:*

Old Katy was a heavy, ugly, short and rough old german woman, with a strange distorted german-english all her own. Anna was worn out now with her attempt to make the younger generation do all that it should and rough old Katy never answered back, and never wanted her own way. No scolding or abuse could make its mark on her uncouth and aged peasant hide. She said her "Yes, Miss Annie," when an answer had to come, and that was always all that she could say. (*The Good Anna,* 17)

Now when her father began fiercely to assail her, she did not really know what it was that he was so furious to force from her. In every way that he could think of in his anger, he tried to make her say a thing she did not really know. She held out and never answered anything he asked her, for Melanctha had a breakneck courage and she just then badly hated her black father.

When the excitement was all over, Melanctha began to know her power, the power she had so often felt stirring within her and which she now knew she could use to make her stronger.

James Herbert did not win this fight with his daughter. After awhile he forgot it as he soon forgot John and the cut of his sharp razor. (*Melanctha,* 95)

The first passage beats steadily, tightly along while the second rushes forward freely and then halts at each "-er" rhyme. The rhymes at the end of each clause support the rhythm, and the rhythm enhances the overall incantatory, hypnotic effect of the repetition.

Related to the repetition and incantatory rhythm, and also to the slightly unconventional word order of *The Good Anna* and *The Gentle Lena,* are the superfluous words (unnecessary for establishing meaning) and commas, very unconventional diction and syntax, introduced in *Melanctha:*

It was very hard for Jeff Campbell to make all this way of doing, right, inside him. If Jeff Campbell could not be straight out, and real honest, he never could be very strong inside him. Now Melanctha,

with her making him feel, always, how good she was and how very
much she suffered in him, made him always go so fast then, he could
not be strong then, to feel things out straight then inside him. Always
now when he was with her, . . . he had something inside him always
holding in him, always now, with her, he was far ahead of his own
feeling. (*Melanctha*, 163)

Stein seems to be carried along by rhythm, hypnotized by her incantation, to the point where her language begins to detach itself
from what it says. This detachment of language from referential
meaning, embryonic in *Melanctha*, is the beginning of Stein's
journey into experimental writing.

The relationship between writing and meaning is transformed
in *Melanctha* in another way: the ordinary, simple vocabulary,
even more reduced than in the earlier novellas, is often used so
elastically, to cover so many meanings, and at the same time so
indeterminately, that certain words become emblematic, invok-
ing large, open-ended complexes of feeling and association, as
well as meaning, each time they appear. These complexes of feeling, association, and meaning remain vague, inchoate; strongly
felt by the reader but never clearly articulated by the narrator.
Each word or phrase increases in significance as it passes through
successive contexts; as its familiar, everyday meanings are gradually replaced by a large complex or cluster of undefined meanings. There are many such key emblematic words in *Melanctha*:
"wisdom," "understanding," "experience," "excitement," being
"quiet together." "Wisdom" becomes an emblem of everything in
life that is desirable but difficult to attain; "excitement" of everything that is alluring but dangerous. We begin to lose our linguistic moorings, the illusion of stability, clarity, firmness of symbolic language which allows us the mastery required by our
everyday lives in patriarchal culture.

Stein's very success in rendering in language a unique core of
personality leads her away from recognizable depiction of character. In *Melanctha*, it is the wavelike cadence and the repetition
of a reduced, strangely resonant and at the same time simple,
childlike vocabulary that hold our attention most forcefully as
we read, beyond our recognition of character, anticipation of

plot, or reflection upon theme. Stein's impulse to alter conventional language in the service of realizing the essence of her subject leads her to abandon coherent thematic treatment of that subject in preference for the possibility of reinventing the structure of thought itself.

CHAPTER 3

Insistence

*And so let us think seriously of the difference between repetition
and insistence. ("Portraits and Repetition," Lectures in America,
167)*

T*hree Lives* is the last of Stein's works until the late twenties
for which it is relevant to give an extended, detailed, full-
blown reading; it is the last real book, or cohesive work *about*
something until *Lucy Church Amiably* and *Four Saints in Three
Acts.* Until the end of Chapter 7, I will not be offering readings, in
any standard sense, of Stein's works. Instead, I will be offering
analyses of the characteristic concatenations of language and
meaning in each of her experimental styles.

Stein's experimental work between *Three Lives* (1906) and *Stanzas in Meditation* (1932) can readily be divided, like a painter's,
into a chronological progression of those styles. After *Melanctha,* Stein's work became increasingly repetitive and incantatory
—what she thought of as "insistent." By 1912, she had transformed this "insistence" into the highly experimental style of *Tender Buttons,* a style I call "lively words," a phrase Stein used in
Lectures in America. The "lively words" (one of Stein's most successful styles) ended in 1914, with the onset of World War I: like
this century, with which Stein was so in tune, her experimental

period was divided by World War I into two discontinuous phases. In 1914, the tight verbal configurations of "lively words" suddenly broke apart. The relatively small amount of work Stein did during and shortly after the war was constructed loosely out of fragments of conversation, of voices. The energized density of the "lively words" was gone, but the open structures of the new style enabled Stein to play with ideas: to add new effects to her medleys of voices. In a synthesis of these and her prewar styles, Stein gradually built the versatile, complex style of the mid-twenties, the style of *Four Saints in Three Acts*.

That no critic consistently studies Stein's radically experimental work by chronological style rather by book or genre is a measure of Stein's success in projecting an image of herself as a mainstream writer who wrote books, in classical genres, with titles; a myth that was probably necessary to her fragile sense of legitimacy, of having a right to be taken seriously. Sutherland divides Stein's work into "stylistic periods," but they are more metaphysical and generic than organic or chronological.[1] Bridgman discusses the first three styles, but does not use them as a basis for criticism, choosing rather to follow Stein's other critics in according the published works of this period an organic unity they do not have.[2] The continuity in the "continuous" prose narratives of 1906-12 (*The Making of Americans, A Long Gay Book, Many Many Women, Matisse, Picasso and Gertrude Stein* [or *G.M.P.*]) is a fiction, a convention of printing. All but one of them (*Many Many Women*) span several styles; and style, not book or genre, is the organizing principle of Stein's experimental work. The last chapter of *The Making of Americans* has more in common with *Many Many Women*, written at the same time, than it does with its own earlier chapters. The collections of Stein's post-1908 work, published both in her lifetime (*Geography and Plays, Portraits and Prayers, Operas and Plays*), and posthumously, in *Last Operas and Plays* and the eight-volume *Yale Edition of the Unpublished Works of Gertrude Stein*, edited by Carl Van Vechten (*Two, Bee Time Vine, Painted Lace*, etc.), have no more real coherence than the long experimental narratives. In general, the published volumes give an impression of a chaotic *oeuvre*; an inaccurate impression, readily corrected by a chronological reading of Stein's work by date of authorship rather than publication.[3] The awkwardness of such a reading (a dozen books piled in front of one, a finger glued to the chronological list of works) is amply recompensed by the order it reveals.

The Making of Americans began as a concerted novelistic project: to "explain" America (the American novelistic project) by tracing the history of two immigrant families, the Herslands and the Dehnings, barely fictionalized versions of Stein's own extended family. But by the middle of the book, as Stein's preoccupations changed, her original project was lost. It was replaced for a time by the confusing, obsessive psychological typology of "bottom natures" ("dependent/independent" and "independent/dependent"), through which Stein hoped to write the "history" of all human beings. But to have a project of such impossible scope was essentially to have none at all. Toward the end of the book, she gradually freed herself from the compulsive, sterile psychological categories, allowing her writing to become primarily incantatory: a language in oblique relationship to referential meaning.

In 1908, she put The Making of Americans aside temporarily to begin A Long Gay Book, nominally a "history" of people in pairs and groups; but one would never know it from most of the text.[4] As in The Making of Americans, the ambitious theme gradually evaporated. Even in her most radical experimental writing, however, Stein always needed subjects to focus her work and give her a beginning. Along with titles and genres, they grounded and solidified her writing, allowing the reader an entrance into many of her most radical works. Unfortunately, the overly ambitious subjects of The Making of Americans and A Long Gay Book have made Stein seem deluded, irresponsible, the fool of a bloated ego. She seems less so, however, when we put her in both psychological and historical context. The scope of the early projects is partly an expression of Stein's neurosis: the familiar dialectic of deep insecurity and megalomania. But it is also essentially similar to the giant modernist projects of the day, barely a caricature of them. What could be more ambitious than to conquer time, or to forge the uncreated conscience of a race?

Throughout the period of "insistence," but at no other time

during her career, Stein recorded regularly in notebooks her plans and ideas for her work; lengthy, intricate analyses of friends and relatives; and also a certain amount of self-analysis and confession.[5] The psychological analyses in the notebooks, as in the fiction they fed, are remarkable for their unflagging intricacy and persistence. Stein had a Talmudic penchant for the fine distinction: for complex, shifting analysis of concatenations of dominant and recessive features both within individuals and among the numerous, overlapping groupings she continually formed and reformed among her friends. But the notebooks are even more remarkable, given what Stein was doing at the time in her literary work, for containing virtually no references to style: they concern only prospective character, plot, and theme. Moreover, though the writing in the notebooks is elliptical and relatively unpunctuated (but no more so than the personal shorthand of much other "private" writing), it is otherwise perfectly conventional, in startling contrast to the drafts of passages for *The Making of Americans* which sporadically appear.

The material in these notebooks has been used by Stein critics both to verify, through evidence of her intention, their thematic interpretations of Stein's works in this period, and also to demonstrate that her primary interest in writing was to communicate her insights into the psychological makeup of the people she knew, her subjects. The notebooks certainly do give the impression of exclusive interest in psychology and character typology, and the concomitant impression that the style of "insistence" must have been unconscious, natural, necessary — of secondary interest and importance to Stein as she wrote, at least in this period.

It is possible to read the evidence of the notebooks quite differently, first by being wary of unwarranted assumptions about the relationship between such notebooks and actual works of literature. The notebooks certainly reveal Stein's interest in and commitment to the material they contain, but they do not prove that she had the same overriding interest in or commitment to that material as she wrote her literary work. It is equally possible that she devoted her full energy and attention to her tortuous analyses in the notebooks precisely so that she would be free to focus her attention, her best effort, elsewhere — on style — in her literary writing. One remark in the notebooks — one of the few directly relevant to composition rather than content — suggests this conclusion: "Writing books is like washing hair you got to soap it a lot of times before you start to rinse it."[6] Perhaps the notebooks existed to allow Stein the many "soapings" she felt necessary before she could "rinse" her material into literary writing.

And in fact, what could be more striking evidence of the conscious intentionality of Stein's stylistic innovation than the discrepancy between the style of the notes and that of the literary writing, so clear in the juxtaposed styles of the notebook itself and of draft passages for the novel? The notes give evidence that she was capable of expressing her ideas, her analyses, her observations in a conventional style: that she considered such conventional expression adequate to a truthful rendering of her intended content, but not adequate to her intentions for literature.

The notebooks also provide dramatic verification of the hypothesis that Stein gradually lost interest in coherent, referential meaning, even as literary fodder. The bulk of the notebooks come from the first part of the "insistent" period, approximately 1906–09, almost entirely devoted to the early sections of *The Making of Americans*. Proportionately little material is devoted to *A Long Gay Book* and the end of *The Making of Americans*, and then, along with "insistence" and coherent, referential meaning itself, the notebooks suddenly stop.

A digression concerning method: the works I discuss in this and the following chapters are not necessarily the best works in each style. They are a compromise between the best and the typical, not uniformly excellent; because I am interested in what makes Stein's experimental writing succeed, I am also interested in what makes it fail.

I will not examine in depth any of the long works of the "insistent" style. They contain passages which are as good as anything else in that style, but to treat any of them adequately as a whole is an arduous and unrewarding task. The same writing is readily accessible in shorter, more manageable works, which are also, on the whole, of higher quality than the wildly uneven long books. Until Stein discovers the free, open structures of her mid-twenties work, which allow her to write long pieces with great success, it is only in the short pieces that we can find consistently good writing. Like various styles of abstract painting, each of Stein's styles dictates an ideal "size," or length of work; and in her early experimental period, that length is short. It is longer in the twenties, and longer still in the final, more conventional phase of 1932–46, whose characteristic genres are the long prose narrative and the full-length play.

The "insistent" style, roughly 1906–11, is an extension of the techniques Stein discovered in *Melanctha:* a reduced, simple vocabulary, emblematic keywords, incantatory rhythm, and above all, repetition. Along with these goes the inevitable diminution in importance of plot, theme, and character — and also, for Stein, of coherent, referential meaning.

Stein continued to be interested in lives, but increasingly she was interested in them as "portraits" — essences of personality, transcending time — rather than as stories. During the first part of *The Making of Americans* (1906–08), she gradually lost the sense of a narrative line. She came to prefer the aloof, intellectualized abstraction initiated in *Three Lives* to the material texture of realistic narrative which makes *Three Lives* palatable to most readers. The pressure to generalize about universal human types overcame her intention to write the history of two particular families, as the static, unchanging essence of a character's "bottom nature," revealed through repetition, replaced the complex discontinuity of a character's life, revealed through accretion of detail in time.

"Bottom nature" can be discerned only by "some one" (Stein) who knows how to listen for repetition, and whose own "bottom nature" is to love it. She describes herself as "having loving repeating as being to a completed understanding"[7]:

Some slowly come to be repeating louder and more clearly the bottom
being that makes them. Listening to repeating, knowing being in
every one who ever was or is or will be living slowly came to be in
me a louder and louder pounding. Now I have it to my feeling to feel
all living, to be always listening to the slightest changing, to have
each one come to be a whole one to me from the repeating in each

one that sometime I come to be understanding. (*The Making of Americans*, 218)

"Slightest changing" is an important phrase. The "insistent" portraits have no development, in the conventional sense, and are designed to reveal an abstract, immutable essence of personality rather than the character change which is the structural basis of realistic fiction. But the notion of change-in-time, "slightest changing," is central to Steinian repetition, and is in fact what makes it "insistence" rather than *mere* repetition:

> There are then many things every one has in them that come out of them in the repeating everything living have always in them, repeating with a little changing just enough to make of each one an individual being, to make of each repeating an individual thing that gives to such a one a feeling of themselves inside them. . . . many millions are always all through their living copying their own repeating, some have this in them because they are indolent in living, it is easier for such of them just to go on with an automatic copying of their own repeating rather than really live inside them their repeating. (*The Making of Americans*, 132)

This argument is the same as the one Stein gives in "Portraits and Repetition" (in *Lectures in America*). To recapitulate that crucial argument yet again, she likens her method to that of the cinema, where the eye of the camera opens on its subject every split second as if seeing it for the first time. The subject itself changes only minutely between shots. Each "frame," or syntactical unit, contains a slightly new emphasis; it is created in a uniquely new moment, part of a "continuous present," with no "memory" of what has come before. This steady, minute shifting in Stein's language, and in her subject's expression of "bottom nature" — re-creation rather than reiteration — is the sign of vitality and authenticity. Its absence is the sign of sterility, "automatic copying": blank silence, inorganic death. Stein equates authentic writing with authentic living; repetition is dead living and writing, "insistence," is live living and writing: "Now I have it to my feeling to feel all living, to be always listening to the slightest changing, to have

each one come to be a whole one to me from the repeating in each
one that sometime I come to be understanding."

"Insistent," incantatory repetition, initiated in *Melanctha*, becomes the hallmark of the 1908–11 style. The present participles,
gerunds and progressive verb forms ("-ing words") which also appear first, marginally, in *Melanctha*, buttress the "continuous
present" with their strong signification of process. The "insistent"
style is an intensification and fusion of the innovations of *Melanctha*, after everything else has been stripped away: the "extra
words" are crucial to the incantatory effect, and the reduced, emblematic vocabulary is just as essential to the style as the "insistent" repetition itself.

"Rue de Rennes," titled with the name of a street near the
Steins' by now (1908) famous house on the rue de Fleurus, is an
interesting early portrait:

In telling again and again that something is frightening some one
that one is convincing some other one that that one is frightened by
that thing and it is a thing that would not be frightening any one, of
that every one is certain. Every one is certain that not any one is
frightened by a thing that is frightening some one. And that one the
one that is frightened by that thing would be frightened by that thing
if that one were feeling certain that that thing is really existing. That
thing is really existing, every one is certain of that thing that that
thing is really existing and so the one that would be frightened by that
thing is frightened by that thing.

That thing is something really existing, to some it is a dreary thing,
to some it is a dirty thing, to some it is a solid thing, to some it is a
noble thing, to some it is a steady thing, to some it is a common thing,
to some it is a simple thing, to some it is an important thing, to some it is
a pleasant thing, to some it is an ugly thing, to some it is a charming
thing, to some it is a serene thing, to some it is a troubled thing, to some
it is a sturdy thing, to some it is the only complete thing, to some one
it is a frightening thing. This thing that is such a thing, this thing that
is existing, that is a frightening thing to one, is a way of living of very
many being living, a way of living of some who are being ones
steadily working, who are ones steadily saving, who are ones paying
what they are always needing to be paying that is enough to be ones
going on being living, who are doing what every one who is of them

First page of the manuscript of "Rue de Rennes." Courtesy of the Yale Collection of American Literature, Beinecke Rare Book and Manuscript Library, Yale University.

is needing so that each one of them can be one going on in being
living, who are ones certainly not needing to be using anything that is
not something they are completely needing to be ones going on being
living, who are ones certainly remembering anything that is a thing
each one of them, any one of them, is needing to be going on in being
living, who are ones certainly not needing to be giving anything for
any one to be remembering anything for any one of them.

Very many are certainly being ones being living and are being ones
going on in being living and certainly this is frightening to some one.
Very many are certainly being ones being living and are being ones
going on being living and some of such of them are not then going on
being living and are not then being living. This is certainly entirely
frightening some one. Very many are certainly being ones being living
and are ones going on being living and they are ones then sometime
not going on being living and are ones then sometime not being living
and some of such of them are ones completely earning and completely
saving and completely using and completely acting to be ones being
such ones and this certainly is frightening some one and this one is
telling again and again that this one is frightened at such of them
being ones being really existing and certainly such of them are ones
being existing. Every one is certain that such of them are ones being
existing. Certainly not any one is believing that such ones being
existing is frightening any one. Certainly every one is certain that not
any one is being frightened by such ones being existing. Some one is
frightened by such ones being existing and is telling it again and
again.[8]

The reduction of vocabulary is immediately apparent in this
litany of a few simple words and phrases: "some one" is "telling
again and again" of being "frightened" by a "thing" that has to do
with "very many" who are "going on being living." These words
and phrases typify the vagueness and generality of Stein's vocabulary in this period, and also of this particular portrait: instead of
specific people performing recognizable actions or moving
through visualizable settings, we have "one" who is "frightened"
and "very many" who are "going on being living." With the exception of "frightened," which is the crucial anchor or focus of this
piece, these words and phrases are the mainstay of the "insistent"
style. They appear everywhere, and in the last years of the style
(1910–11), "one" and "going on being living," along with a few

other phrases, overwhelm the writing, making it virtually un-readable (see particularly *Many Many Women*).

Stein acknowledges both the reduction and the vague general-ity of this vocabulary in the "Alfred Hersland" chapter of *The Making of Americans*:

> To be using a new word in my writing is to me a very difficult thing. Every word I am ever using in writing has for me very existing being. . . . I like one I am very fond of that one one that has many meanings many ways of being used to make different meanings to every one. . . . I may know very well the meaning of a word and yet it has not for me completely weight and form and really existing being. There are only a few words and with these mostly always I am writing that have for me completely entirely existing being, in talking I use many more of them of words I am not living but talking is another thing, . . . often then I am using many words I never could be using in writing. (306)

The few words that have "really existing being" have "many meanings many ways of being used to make different meanings to every one." That is precisely what the emblematic words in *Melanctha* ("wisdom," "excitement," etc.) were, only in the "insis-tent" style they have become almost entirely disembodied, de-prived of the complex of reference and association, however un-defined and open-ended, accumulated in the course of a story. They are emblematic words whose large clusters of reference are a mystery. Stein's commitment to them, her almost liturgical use of them, endows them with importance, with the aura of pro-found significance. But there is no contextual history to elevate or expand them beyond their barest intelligibility. The writing seems a negation of everything one values in literature. But it need not be, if the reader is willing to collaborate fully with the writer in generating the text.

In successful "insistence," Stein provides a skeleton of coher-ent, referential meaning, which the reader must flesh out accord-ing to his or her imagination and experience, as in Barthes's "writerly" text, where the reader shares equally with the author the work of writing:

Why is the writerly our value? Because the goal of literary work (of literature as work) is to make the reader no longer a consumer, but a producer of the text. Our literature is characterized by the pitiless divorce which the literary institution maintains between the producer of the text and its user, between its owner and its customer, between its author and its reader. This reader is thereby plunged into a kind of idleness . . . instead of functioning himself, instead of gaining access to the magic of the signifier, to the pleasure of writing, he is left with no more than the poor freedom either to accept or reject the text: reading is nothing more than a *referendum*.[9]

Stein's responsibility is to make this core of meaning capable of evoking and supporting private layers of association. The vocabulary with which she builds and elaborates this meaning must not only have "really existing being" for her; it must be capable of having "really existing being" for her reader. It must indeed have "many meanings many ways of being used to make different meanings to *every one*." The writing in this style fails precisely when it has no underpinning or core meaning, when it gives itself up completely to repetition of words that have "really existing being" only for Stein. Such writing would deny the reader not only the possibility of active, imaginative participation in the creation of the text, but of reading it at all. This necessary core of meaning is conventionally coherent and referential, but the way it actually functions in the text is not.

The first sentence of "Rue de Rennes" establishes the essential skeleton of meaning which Stein will elaborate throughout the portrait: "something is frightening some one." It also establishes the boundaries of content, simultaneously giving the core of the portrait and warning that this is all the solid information one can expect. The reader who resists, who reads on impatiently, waiting for illumination (what is "something," who is "some one") will be dismayed. The reader must instead embrace the ambiguity and indeterminacy of the text, letting her or his imagination play over the core meaning, forming associations, calling up sympathetic experience. This activity is always part of reading, but it is generally peripheral or subliminal: most readers are conditioned to acknowledge as they read only what is "*in*" the text; they fail to recognize or validate the idiosyncratic images, feelings, and recollections *evoked by* it.

"In telling again and again that something is frightening some one that one is convincing some other one that that one is frightened by that thing and it is a thing that would not be frightening any one, of that every one is certain." At the center of the portrait are a protagonist ("some one") and an object or phenomenon (a "thing" or "something") which is "frightening" the protagonist: a subject, an object, and a relationship between them. This is a sufficiently solid, clear core of meaning. "Some one" and "something" are the typically blank, neutral words of "insistence," referring to specific people or objects without naming them.[10] They dictate no particular reference, but are pliable and familiar enough to be ready vehicles for the association triggered in the reader by the relationship of fear between them. The rest of the text achieves signification *in conjunction with* the central assertion of the portrait: "something is frightening some one." The word "frightening," loaded as it is, establishes an emotional tone, locating or anchoring the piece, giving the reader a cue for imagination and association. The reader must hold this cue in mind as it is carried through the various permutations and modifications that constitute the body of the portrait.

Without its core of meaning, "Rue de Rennes" would be difficult to read at all. A good deal of it, particularly the long third paragraph, would be typical of the worst of the "insistent" style — blank, nonsignifying, dead, such as the following:

He who was one and all and all were then, he and he was one and all who were some were then, he and all and he and some, they were all and he was one and all and all were then and he was one, and all and he and all were and he was one, and all were who were and all were . . .[11]

The knowledge that the "thing" discussed in the second and third paragraphs is "frightening some one" enables us to read that discussion by placing some limitation on the boundaries of possible meaning, allowing the writing to become incantation rather than bewildering repetition. The primary effect of the writing comes from its aural features. If we had to struggle to understand the referential meaning, as we would without the notion of fear, the incantatory effect would be vitiated. We would come away only with an unsatisfying interpretation of thematic content — unsatisfying because it is the least interesting element of the work.

Once limits are placed on the possibilities of signification, once we have a solid core of referential meaning firmly lodged in our minds, the rest of the meanings come to us as we read without struggle. We are free to lose ourselves in the incantation, which, as long as it is accompanied by referential meaning, is the primary and most rewarding feature of this work, of "insistence." Without some referential meaning, we lose the incantation; without the incantation, the referential meaning is not worth having.

We can interpret "Rue de Rennes" quite coherently, but I do not think such interpretation would be possible without the core of the piece: "some one" being "frightened" by "something." In the second paragraph, we find out that "something" is "a way of living to very many being living," which involves "steadily working" and "steadily saving," "paying," and "using" only what is absolutely necessary to "be ones going on being living," never "giving anything for any one" to do ("remember") anything (household work, for example). The tightfisted, lower-middle-class life that Stein depicted in *The Good Anna* and *The Gentle Lena* immediately comes to mind. It was clear in those novellas that Stein was indeed "frightened" of that sort of life: it literally killed Anna, and it steadily wrung the life out of Lena. But without the knowledge that "someone" is afraid of this way of life, we would have to dig for this meaning, engaging our rational, analytical faculties so exclusively that the incantatory effect would be lost.

If a reader began, for example, at the second sentence of the second paragraph, omitting the crucial phrase "that is a frightening thing to one," the writing would seem so arbitrary that no meaning would penetrate at all. The reader would lose the effect of the incantation in the urgency of simply understanding what he or she read. The meaning the reader would finally arrive at would seem thin, simple, and insignificant. The reader might well feel put upon: the fruits of this difficult reading would in no way reward the effort.

Again, as long as the core of referential meaning is clear enough (though always abstract, unfixed, allowing each reader to "make different meanings"), we are free to allow meaning to recede, as it should in this writing, behind incantation, which is the real "point" of "insistence." In successful "insistence," as opposed to the later, *fully* experimental writing, language is pulled away, rather than detached, from coherent, referential meaning: such meaning is present in the text, but it is separate from the primary effect of the words as they are read.

Successful "insistent" writing need not be limited to a single core of meaning. Though "Rue de Rennes" is not the only successful portrait with a single core,[12] other successful portraits, as well as passages from the longer works, are characterized by what are in effect a series of related cores.[13] Stein's very first portrait, "Ada" (1908), whose subject is Alice Toklas, weaves together several key observations about Toklas's life and personality, about her relationship with Stein, and about Stein's feelings toward her:

Ada was then one and all her living then one completely telling stories that were charming, completely listening to stories having a beginning and a middle and an ending. Trembling was all living, living was all loving, some one was then the other one. Certainly this one was loving this Ada then. And certainly Ada all her living then was happier in living than any one else who ever could, who was, who is, who ever will be living. (*Geography and Plays*, 16)

"Two: Gertrude Stein and her Brother" (1910–12) is another successful work with a number of related cores. Its central motif is "sound coming out" of "him" or "her," but this is interwoven with "listening," "creating," "feeling," "expressing," and a number of other Steinian indices of character.

When there are too many unrelated points or cores of meaning, the writing becomes chaotic, as in "Russell," "Pach" or "Hessel."[14] However, the most characteristic problem of the "insistent" writing is not a superfluity of unintegrated observation, but rather the opacity and blandness of the vocabulary on which the burden of establishing the core of meaning rests. After "insistence," coherent, referential meaning is gone. But in the period of "insistence," Stein always works with some core of meaning: she always makes some point about her subject. Nonetheless, these points are frequently blotted out by the generality of the language she uses to make them; for example: "They were each one of them knowing that succeeding in living is something that is completely existing."[15]

In subordinating meaning to incantation as radically as she does in "insistence," Stein shifts the domain of literary experience from the rational, ordering, interpreting mode of symbolic language to what might be called a meditative mode — stiller, slower, less aggressive, less ordering — which is presymbolic in its foregrounding of the aural features of language. This peaceful mode is also associated with various forms of meditation, yoga, and relaxation, and also with listening to music. All of these have in common with Stein's "insistent" writing the predominance of a repetitive rhythm. That rhythm is essential to the slowing down of consciousness which permits the transition to the meditative state. The repetitiveness of the vocabulary and syntax of "insistence," which generate the steady wavelike rhythm, and the moment-by-moment shifting of emphasis of the "continuous present," work together to slow the reader's mental time. If this writing is to be read at all, it must be read with concentration — much more than conventional prose demands — and also slowly, moment by moment. We cannot race through "what we already know she's going to say" to "find out what happens next." The meaninglessness and colorlessness of the repeated words, like that of meditation mantras, free the mind from active rationality, allowing it to become simultaneously concentrated and still.

In "Rue de Rennes," the high incantation of the second sentence in the second paragraph comes at just the right moment in the development of the piece. The reader is drawn into the writing, given a narrative foothold. With meaning accounted for in the first paragraph, the writing is free to become incantatory, and the reader's mind is free to enter the meditative state.

The incantation of "Rue de Rennes," unlike most of the "insistent" incantation, is contained within a closed circular form, very similar to certain musical structures.[16] The piece owes much of its effectiveness to that structure. There is an initial theme (what I have called the core of meaning), which is gradually elaborated and modified, as the piece moves farther from its origin. At a certain point, midway through the piece or toward the end (in "Rue de Rennes," the middle of the third paragraph), the threads are gathered together, and the initial theme is recapitulated, transformed in "Rue de Rennes" by the distance it has travelled from nervous assertion to relieved affirmation.

The musical analogy is neither new nor gratuitous. With its careful permutation of syntax, its emphasis on rhythm, and its utter dependence on movement through time, the "insistent" style has always appeared musical, even apart from its affinity with music in producing a meditative state. That familiar musical analogy can be extended to illuminate the most difficult features of the "insistent" style: the bare colorlessness of the heavily repeated vocabulary, the exaggerated simplicity of the syntax, and the mechanical predictability of the permutations which produce the "insistent" repetition. The musical analogy allows us to account for Stein's perverse denial of the richness, color and variety of the language as a kind of atonalism, whose purpose is to rescue tonality from the excesses of romanticism (in *The Autobiography of Alice B. Toklas*, she says her aim as a writer has been the "destruction of associational emotion"). But rather than destroying the nuance, texture, emotional subtlety, and richness of association of the language, Stein, like the modernist poets, is actually trying to save them — not only by paring away all but the purest elements, but also by actually working against them; clarifying and even sacralizing them by insisting upon their opposite, emphasizing them through their absence, or, in a favored twentieth-century version of the paradox, preserving them by destroying them. Stein's feeling toward words is reverential. Throughout her experimental period she composes a liturgy for the religion of language. As she says in a notebook, "I believe in repetition. Yes. Always and always, Must write the hymn of repetition."[17]

CHAPTER 4

Lively Words

. . .the words have the liveliness of being constantly chosen.
("What is English Literature," Lectures in America, 25)

In 1910–11, as she was finishing *The Making of Americans* and beginning *Many Many Women*, *G.M.P.*, and *A Long Gay Book*, Stein's writing progressively detached itself from coherent referential meaning, becoming pure incantation. But, as we have seen, the success of the "insistent" style depends on the presence of some such meaning in the text. Late "insistent" writing moves very far in the direction of blank nonsignification:

She in satisfying every one was satisfying every one that she was
some one and in satisfying every one in satisfying every one that she
was some one was satisfying every one that she was some one and in
satisfying every one that she was some one she was one who was, in
satisfying every one that she was some one, was satisfying every one
that she was some one.[1]

This is "automatic copying," dead by Stein's own definition. There is no organic growth from phrase to phrase; no momentum; no shifting, multiple possibility of meaning; there is only the inane, nonsignifying reiteration of a broken record.

Sometime in 1911, Stein began to write differently.[2] The "-ing words" receded, the incessant pounding of the incantatory rhythm faded; "one" and its sibling pronouns virtually disappeared, replaced by more and more interesting "new words." The change in style is startlingly clear in the "Portrait of Constance Fletcher," circa 1911. Its first page and a half are in the "insistent" style, and then, using a different manuscript notebook, Stein suddenly starts writing in a new way:

She was filling in in all her living to be a full one, she was thinking and feeling in all her living in being a full one. She was thinking and feeling all her living in being one who could be a completely full one. She was all her living a full one. She was completely filling in to be a full one and she always was a full one. She was thinking in being a full one. She was feeling in being a full one. She was thinking in feeling in being a full one. She was feeling in thinking in being a full one.
If they move in the shoe there is everything to do. They do not move in the shoe.
The language of education is not replacing the special position that is the expression of the emanation of evil. There is an expression when contemplation is not connecting the object that is in position with the forehead that is returning looking. It is not overpowering. That is a cruel description. The memory is the same and surely the one who is not older is not dead yet although if he has been blind he is seeing. This has not any meaning.
Oh the bells that are the same are not stirring and the languid grace is not out of place and the older fur is disappearing. There is not such an end.
If it had happened that the little flower was larger and the white color was deeper and the silent light was darker and the passage was rougher it would have been as it was and the triumph was in the place where the light was bright and the beauty was not losing having that possession. That was not what was tenderly. This was the piece of the health that was strange when there was the disappearance that had not any origin. The darkness was not the same. There was the writing and the preparation that was pleasing and succeeding and being enterprising. It was not subdued when there was discussion, it was done where there was the room that was not a dream.[3]

Stein probably put this portrait aside, returning to it months later with a changed style. Similar transitions can be found in *A*

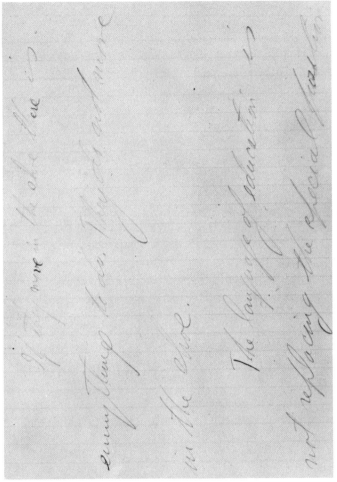

Manuscript page from "Portrait of Constance Fletcher." Courtesy of the Yale Collection of American Literature, Beinecke Rare Book and Manuscript Library, Yale University.

65

Long Gay Book and *G.M.P.*, where the shift from one style to the next is more gradual than in the "Portrait of Constance Fletcher," and one can watch the new style emerge: colorful, concrete adjectives and nouns appear in place of the privileged gerunds and participles, and simple present or past tense in place of the ubiquitous progressives. Stein also begins moving on to something new in each phrase instead of recasting the previous one: creating a "continuous present" is no longer important. She retains, at first, the simple, repetitive syntax which was the skeleton of the "insistent" style — relying heavily, as in the passage from "Portrait of Constance Fletcher," on "if . . . then" formulations, simple predicate sentences with various conjugations of "to be," arbitrary alternations of assertion and negation and of question and answer, and additive lists ("all this makes a _____").

"If they move in the shoe there is everything to do" seems to have *nothing* to do with "she was filling in in all her living to be a full one." Not only is the language varied and colorful instead of bland and monotonous; the tone is expansive, light, and joyful rather than dry, heavy, and obsessive. Instead of strong continuity from phrase to phrase, with painfully small shifts of emphasis, there is no continuity whatever. Where the "insistent" style, when successful, retained a core of referential meaning, the new style completely confounds conventional reading: "This has not any meaning." Writing that sentence in "Portrait of Constance Fletcher" seems to have given Stein such a burst of energy and joy that she began the next sentence "Oh the bells."

Many aesthetic theories, which apply equally well to radical or avant-garde forms in any of the arts, have been invoked to explain this fully experimental writing. Twentieth-century art must reflect the new fragmented twentieth-century reality, with its subjectivist epistemology, its emphasis on nonrational areas of the mind, its notion of consciousness as a chaotic flow of private association, its vision of events as acausal, of time as nonlinear, of truth and reality as plural and undetermined. Moreover, art is no longer seen as primarily representational or mimetic. It is instead autonomous, responsible to its own formal dimensions, important as the source of the privileged aesthetic experience rather than as an instructive mimesis of life.

In "Portraits and Repetition" (*Lectures in America*), Stein explains *Tender Buttons,* the central work of "lively words," as an attempt to re-create her still-life subjects in pure language, using not words that "mean it" but words that are "equivalent to it." That statement is premised on the central avant-garde notion of the autonomy or purity of the artistic medium, a notion which transforms the relation of art to reality from imitation or mirroring to reinvention. Art re-creates a subject in "pure" paint, sound, or words.

Stein's critics have given us numerous amplifications of her account. Bridgman explains *Tender Buttons* as a continuum of private association which is everyone's *real* experience of the external world; as a product of the freed imagination, its deepest material rising to the surface from the recesses of the unconscious mind, bursting forth in liberated vocabulary. Sutherland invokes the fusion of "insides and outsides"—outer reality expressed in terms of inner reality—and also Stein's religious sense of the physical plenitude of the world, of life as an immediate, physical, moment-to-moment miracle which can be captured only in a special language—a religious sense which is the source of her affinity with saints. Stewart interprets, finding Jungian archetypes. Weinstein gives us linguistic relativism, the subjectivity of perception, James's notion of language as a falsifier of mental reality. He sees *Tender Buttons,* and all of Stein's experimental work, as an attempt to express in language the areas of consciousness language normally ignores, to delineate the true contours of the mind, and to create an autonomous, plastic literature. In one of the most important studies of *Tender Buttons,* "Gertrude Stein as Post-Modernist: The Rhetoric of *Tender Buttons,*" Neil Schmitz properly locates the work as a harbinger of contemporary postmodernism in that it calls into question—as does the work of Borges, Robbe-Grillet, Beckett, Barth, Barthelme, Burroughs, Brautigan—our defining notions of language, narrative, literature, and ultimately, the world.[4] But how do we read this writing? Where in it does meaning reside, what are the dimensions of that meaning, how does it reach us, and how is it generated?

"If they move in the shoe there is everything to do. They do not move in the shoe." Those two simple, playful sentences, which initiate the new style in "Portrait of Constance Fletcher," can be used critically as an exemplum of Stein's early "lively words." These sentences are both effective and typical; any number of other fragments from the writing of this period could be analyzed in the same way. There is no coherent, referential meaning in them, but they are dense with multiple, open-ended connections of lexical meaning (image, association, connotation, resonance). At the same time, they function powerfully at the level of the signifier, through sound and rhythm. This successful combination of pluridimensional and presymbolic signification makes "lively words" one of the best examples yet produced of experimental writing as anti-patriarchal language. The "lively words," much more than the bland vocabulary of "insistence," (a vocabulary which generates a stillness in the reader's mind rather than an energized flood of images), have "many meanings many ways of being used to make different meanings to every one." In "lively words" lexical meaning, syntactical structure, and sound and rhythm patterns are all activated separately — sometimes harmonically, sometimes dissonantly. In the two sentences from "Portrait of Constance Fletcher," syntax is at odds with sound and rhythm, contributing an extra level of signification.

The sound and rhythm are strongly evocative of lilting nursery rhyme, literally suggesting Mother Goose: "There was an old lady who lived in a shoe" is probably their source. Children's language provides an immediate return to the presymbolic. Stein exploits that primal resonance, and at the same time transforms it into something linguistically more complex.

"Move in the shoe" suggests the old lady and her horde of children. It also suggests a foot, both literally shifting about inside a shoe, and moving, in a shoe, through space. Whatever further images are called up by "move in the shoe" will vary from reader to reader. Their precise content is irrelevant. What matters is their structure: disembodied, dreamlike, these images are evoked simultaneously, none clear, full, or consistent, but all with the eerie plausibility of surrealist painting. If the complexes of meaning, image, and association attached in our minds to the words "move" and "shoe" were incapable of significant relationship, the unusual juxtaposition "move in the shoe" would evoke nothing.

But shoes are naturally associated with moving. The two are consonant enough, in roughly the same semantic world, so that their dissonance is significant rather than totally baffling, just as Magritte's large green apples are troublingly, comically similar to the men's heads they replace. The expectation we have in conventional reading that each word will make sense next to the one before it must be kept aroused in order to be refreshingly disappointed: if it is not aroused, there is no jolt, no excitement, no feeling of a rich new language drawn magically from the tired body of the old. Both the *irreducible* multiplicity (Barthes) and the strangeness of these images are a product of the simultaneous suggestiveness and dissonance of this particular syntactical linkage of "move" and "shoe." One does not normally speak of moving in a shoe, but it is close enough to an acceptable English phrase to be polysemous rather than totally incapable of significance: precisely Chomsky's "second degree of grammaticalness."

Where the "insistent" writing is decelerated to long phrases, this writing is decelerated to short phrases and single words. Each word casts a new light on the word before it, creating a new cluster of images and associations. The reader must literally read one word at a time, not so much in the early "lively words" style of "Portrait of Constance Fletcher," with its bulk of mediating syntax, but in *Tender Buttons* and the portraits of 1913 ("Susie Asado," "Preciosilla," "Guillaume Apollinaire"), where the language becomes powerfully concentrated. The juxtaposition of words is everything in this style. As Stein says, in praise of Elizabethan writing, "it was the specific word next to the specific word next it chosen to be next it that was the important thing" ("What is English Literature,"31). It is in the jostling of word against word, just as much as in the simple vibrance of the words themselves, that this style is "lively."

Stein's successful juxtapositions often rest on the clear visual images provided by concrete nouns. The two sentences from "Portrait of Constance Fletcher" would be less effective without the palpable presence of the shoe. *Tender Buttons* is generally more successful than the earlier portraits, precisely because it eliminates the monotonous syntax and blank vocabulary, and concentrates instead the visually evocative language. Where the "insistent" style was closest to music, "lively words" is closest to painting. "Insistence" depended on the shifting increment of repetition in time; "lively words" depends, like a painting, on static (as much as literature can be static) moments of interrelationship among its semantic elements, one of the most important of which is the visual image. As in cubism and surrealism, commonplace objects are for Stein the most reliable sources of strong and uncorrupted visual imagery. A central preoccupation of Stein's, and of many avant-garde movements and artists, is the attempt to generate a new, anti-literary repertoire of images for art. That is one import of the found objects of cubism and surrealism, and of Robbe-Grillet's famous nonsignifying objects. But beyond that, from "lively words" through "melody," the content of a Steinian experimental text — the actual lexical meaning it articulates — is irrelevant to its effect as writing. "Move in the shoe" is not intended as communication to the reader *about* shoes or moving. It reaches the reader, instead, through anti-patriarchal modes of signification: the pre-Oedipal *jouissance* of the signifier, and the pluridimensionality (multiplicity, incoherence) of those articulations of lexical meaning.

Leo Stein, who hated cubism ("I think cubism whether in painting or ink is tommyrot"), can help us see what makes Stein's "lively words" successful.[5] He wrote a parody of the early "lively words" style, a "criticism" of Gertrude's famous "Portrait of Mabel Dodge at the Villa Curonia":[6]

AN AUTHOR

Size is not circumference unless magnitude extends. Purpose
defined in limitation projected. It is the darkness whose center is light.
Hardly can the movement arrest. Formality is subservience.
Liquidation confluent with purpose by involution elaborates the
elemental. Its significance protracts but virtue is dissimulated.
All men are so but not in all ways. It is the thought process but not
detached. Relations may be elaborated and hence illumination.
Though the mole is blind the earth is one.[7]

This piece is intended to be indistinguishable from Gertrude's writing, but in fact is hardly anything like it. It has none of her force, originality, whimsy or complexity. The language is dry, latinate, pedantically abstract. There are no vivid images, no startling, resonant juxtapositions — only blank, circumlocutory nonsense ("Liquidation confluent with purpose by involution elaborates the elemental") or pretentious pseudo-profundity ("It is the darkness whose center is light." "Though the mole is blind the earth is one"). The purpose of the childish simplicity of Stein's writing is precisely to avoid such heavy pretentiousness.

Leo's failed attempt is indeed an excellent foil for Gertrude's successes. Beyond the blandness and pretentiousness of Leo's piece, its worst failing is the obviousness, to the point of cliché, of his verbal associations: size, circumference, magnitude; darkness and light; movement and arrest; formality and subservience; relations, elaborated, illumination; mole and earth. At the heart of Gertrude's brilliance in "lively words" is her ability to invent unfamiliar, surprising, fresh conjunctions of words, which are nonetheless consonant enough to generate multiple, undetermined meaning (in Chomsky's terminology, deviations from, rather than total disruptions of, conventional grammatic patterns). If we "just let words come," without exercising any control or selectivity, they will come in very familiar patterns, as Leo's did.[8] Gertrude consciously abrogates those familiar patterns, replacing them by suggestive combinations which prevent the normal, orderly, hierarchical functioning of thought-in-language, forcing our thought into the anarchic configurations repressed by patriarchy. Leo superficially abandons conventional meaning but retains the verbal associations, the blocks of language, which are its essential units. Gertrude breaks up those blocks of language, and weaves the liberated fragments in felicitous (joyous, *jouissant*) patterns of sound, image, connotation, and association. Leo's conjunctions, because of their familiarity, seem to mean something, but don't. Gertrude's conjunctions, because of their unfamiliarity, seem to mean nothing, but are richly resonant. Hers has the startling, refreshing, liberating effect of successful subversion, while Leo's has virtually no effect at all.

Syntax contributes to the effect. Though unobtrusive, it is still important — often at odds with sound and rhythm, as in "If they move in the shoe there is everything to do. They do not move in the shoe." The center of these sentences is "move in the shoe." That phrase both supports the nursery rhyme quality of sound and rhythm, and functions by itself as incoherent anti-patriarchal signification. Syntax functions at yet another level, however. Partly, it is the last vestige of the "insistent" style, in its monotonous predictability. There are a few simple syntactical structures which Stein uses repeatedly in this early style, at its worst a game of fill-in-the-blanks: if _____ then _____; _____ is _____ which is _____; _____ is not _____ which makes all of _____; etc. The two sentences from "Portrait of Constance Fletcher" are typical, a conditional followed by a negation: If they _____ in the _____ there is _____. They do not _____. Simply, the predictable syntax is a device for moving the writing along.

But syntax also functions at a deeper level in this writing, as a sort of *trompe l'oeil*. All the syntactical structures of the transitional style are logical, expository, almost argumentative: the grammatical sign of exactly the kind of patriarchal-symbolic writing which Stein subverts here, and vastly different in tone from whimsical phrases such as "move in the shoe." These logical structures work to make us expect coherent meaning. As we have seen, this *expectation* must be aroused for the "lively words" to have their subversive, jolting effect. Moreover, there is an illusion of meaning as well as the arousal of the expectation of meaning, and therein lies the *trompe l'oeil*. This illusion of meaning mocks and confounds the orderly logic of coherent meaning. This mockery is clearest in the arbitrary (and dialectically sophisticated) use of the word "not," as if it doesn't matter at all whether one asserts or negates. As Stein says of marble which is all real instead of partly real and partly false, "there was nothing to content the eye by deceiving it" ("Pictures," 72). In the two sentences from "Portrait of Constance Fletcher," we are "deceived," and perhaps contented, by the pseudo-syllogistic structure, which leaves us with the profound conclusion that there is not, in fact, "everything to do."

Though there are some remnants of bland syntax in the writing of 1912–13, it is largely replaced by a tighter connection of words based on sound association, rhythm patterns, and linkages of lexical meaning of the "second degree of grammaticalness." In

"Portrait of Constance Fletcher," we can isolate the fragments that would probably survive in the later style and those that might not. "The language of education is not replacing the special position that is the expression of the emanation of evil. There is an expression when contemplation is not connecting the object that is in position with the forehead that is returning looking." The first sentence would not survive: though it has the deceptive plausibility and the steady jolt of expectation that characterize the successful writing in this style, the language is too abstract. Except for the glibly, conventionally emotive "emanation of evil," there are no vivid, startling juxtapositions.

The second sentence is in the same mode (as is most of the passage), until we come to the "forehead that is returning looking." Despite its backward-looking "-ing words," that phrase has the same structure as "move in the shoe": a concrete noun connected in an unconventional, semi-grammatical way to a general, suggestive verb or verbal phrase. Just as "move" is readily associated with "shoe," "returning looking" is readily associated with "forehead." Again there is an eerie, open-ended configuration of images (a forehead, two pairs of staring eyes) connected simultaneously, irreducibly in many ways. It is an arresting image, and the writing suddenly comes to life when it appears.

There are other resonant, successful phrases in that passage from "Portrait of Constance Fletcher," such as "cruel description," "the older fur is disappearing," and "the room that was not a dream." "Cruel description" is a startling juxtaposition: the word "description" connotes the neutral, factual, objective, not the "cruel." Yet that phrase resonates deeply through the realms of gossip, criticism, and literature itself. This phrase turns on connotation and association rather than visual imagery, with the emotional and aural impact of "cruel" substituting for the visual impact of a concrete image.

"The older fur is disappearing" is a classic phrase of this style. To a sense-seeking reading it registers as nonsense, because a juxtaposition of these three words is so uncommon, and because, in fact, the phrase makes no conventional, unitary sense. But it does trigger irreducibly numerous images and associations: it suggests both an old coat and an old animal passing out of one's life; it suggests simply hair, or an animal's fur, falling out; it evokes the sexual connotation of "fur," as Stein did in "Miss Furr and Miss Skeene" (17–22). But the comparative form of "old" and the mysterious word "disappearing," in conjunction with the rich word "fur," complicate the phrase, pulling it away from those lurking determinate meanings and making them multiple, openended, undetermined. Paradoxically, the closer this writing comes to conventional usage, the more we *expect* coherence of it, the more disturbingly senseless it seems.

"The room that was not a dream" plays on the closeness of the sounds of "room" and "dream," and also evokes sleeping and dreaming both of and in a room. The "not" is simultaneously a logical, syntactical *trompe l 'oeil*, confounding sense, and also a source of meaning: a room is, literally, not a dream. Insofar as this phrase comes much closer than the others to a conventional use of language, in its emotionally familiar, imagistically "easy" conjunction of room and dream, it is less successful than the other phrases.

These phrases from "Portrait of Constance Fletcher" are typical of the "lively words" writing. Understanding how they function (how to read them, how they offer meaning, what kind of meaning they offer) is all one needs in order to read the other "lively words" writing for oneself, and the point of this writing is precisely that each reader must read it, and therefore help write it, for him- or herself. Again, I do not believe that Stein's experimental writing asks to be interpreted; I do not believe that we need critical works to excavate and order its meanings. I offer these readings of phrases from "Portrait of Constance Fletcher" only as illustrations of this style, not as critical ends in themselves. Another reader would give different readings, as another reader must: this writing is designed to "make different meanings to every one." "Portrait of Constance Fletcher" or *Tender Buttons* are not like *Middlemarch* or *Daniel Deronda*, for which it would certainly not be adequate simply to define the genre "novel," or "Victorian novel," or even "George Eliot novel," interpret a characteristic passage, and invite each reader to proceed from there, feeling one has done all a critic can or should to elucidate them. *Middlemarch* and *Daniel Deronda* cannot be elucidated fully without detailed discussion of their particular configurations of form and meaning.

In addition to its open-ended "writerliness," two further characteristics of Stein's radical experimental work make the critic's task in elucidating it entirely different from that of the George Eliot critic (or the critic of any other conventional writing). Since, again, division of Stein's experimental writing into separate, titled works is much less meaningful than its division into chronological styles, individual works within a particular style are more or less interchangeable. Whereas a paragraph about Dorothea or Casaubon could not possibly be from *Daniel Deronda*, a paragraph from "Portrait of Constance Fletcher" could very easily be from *GMP*, written around the same time, though it could not be from "The King or Something (The Public is Invited to Dance)" written six years later.

Also, coherent, referential meaning — the transcendental signified — is crucial to *Middlemarch* and *Daniel Deronda* and absent from Stein's experimental work. It would be very difficult to take Eliot's novels seriously and avoid interpreting them in order to arrive at a thematic synthesis, or a number of possible thematic syntheses if one is a deconstructionist, unique to each. Stein's radical works deny, avoid, in fact negate the transcendental signified. They have no themes. Interpretation of them — close reading of a whole text — is reduced to listing all possible combinations of lexical meanings, as if those meanings themselves (a foot can move around inside a shoe or a shoe can move through space; gossip can be cruel; hair falls out; a room is different from a dream) were the point of the writing.

I find arguments for the interpretable coherence of *Tender Buttons* particularly unconvincing — straining as they do to see patterns in a genuine chaos (Stewart, for example, sees a "mandala"; Bridgman a "thematic progression") — as well as misleading. The entire thrust of this style, as of Stein's experimental writing in general, is against conventional, unitary coherence, and there is certainly no reason to base thematic syntheses on Stein's notoriously whimsical, arbitrary titles and orderings of her material.

The precise dates of composition of *Tender Buttons* are unclear. The *Yale Catalogue* lists them as 1910–12 but Stein says, in

The Autobiography of Alice B. Toklas, that she began the work during her spring and summer in Spain in 1912, and finished it when she returned to Paris in the fall. She is vague about the order of composition of the three sections, and of the fragments within them. It is my belief, based on manuscript evidence, style, and on what she says in *The Autobiography of Alice B. Toklas,* that the book was organized into its present configuration after it was written.[9] "Rooms," the third section of the book, is all in the 1911, transitional style. It is essentially indistinguishable from "Portrait of Constance Fletcher" or "Portrait of Mabel Dodge at the Villa Curonia": "A shine is that which when covered changes permission";[10] "China is not down when there are plates, lights are not ponderous and incalculable" (*Tender Buttons,* 505); "The care with which there is incredible justice and likeness, all this makes a magnificent asparagus, and also a fountain" (509).

"Objects" and "Food," the first and second sections of the book, both begin in the transitional style, then accelerate steadily through the middle style toward the extreme style of 1913. On the first page of "Objects" we can find a sentence like "It certainly showed no obligation and perhaps if borrowing is not natural there is some use in giving" (461). By the end of "Objects," the writing has become much more fragmented: "Black ink best wheel bale brown. Excellent not a hull house, not a pea soup, no bill, no care, no precise no past pearl pearl goat" (476). The same progression is evident in "Food," which begins: "In the inside there is sleeping, in the outside there is reddening, in the morning there is meaning, in the evening there is feeling" (477). That section ends in a very different style: "Next to me next to a folder, next to a folder some waiter, next to a foldersome waiter and re letter and read her. Read her with her for less" (497).

There is no reason to struggle to interpret or unify either the whole of *Tender Buttons* or any part of it, not only because there is no consistent pattern of meaning, but because we violate the spirit of the work in trying to find one. Like the rest of the "lively words" writing, *Tender Buttons* functions anti-patriarchally: as presymbolic *jouissance* and as irreducibly multiple, fragmented, open-ended articulation of lexical meaning. Its primary modes are dissonance, surprise, play. It mocks the dominating earnest-

ness which would master it, tame it, contain it within a unifying
design. Donald Sutherland is not, as Bridgman implies, shirking
his critical responsibility in calling it, and most of Stein's experimental writing, "a sort of Wonderland or Luna Park for anybody
who is not too busy."[11] Luce Irigaray, in *Ce sexe qui n'en est pas
un*, locates female language on the other side of the looking glass;
Luna Park, accordingly, is a realm of both strangeness and pure
play. The experience of reading "lively words" is precisely Alice's
in Wonderland or anyone's in Luna Park, with the same psychic
density and absolute nonseriousness. In Stein's language, as in
Carroll's dream world, the ordinary is transformed into the startlingly nonordinary without losing its resonant recognizability.
But there is no chess game in *Tender Buttons*. Its clearest link to
the world of patriarchal hierarchy, sense, and coherence—the
titles of its sections and subsections—are the very means by
which Stein mocks and confounds our need for sense and coherence. She uses them exactly the way she used syntax in "Portrait
of Constance Fletcher," to arouse the expectation of sense, give
the illusion of it, and then undermine both.

Most of the subtitles in the "Objects" section have something to
do with real objects, even if the writing does not (some of it does,
even occasionally mentioning the nominal subject of the "still-
life"). The interpreting reader is encouraged, making allowances
for "irrelevant" or "senseless" passages as long as there is some
basic line of coherence to follow. That reader loses heart when,
toward the end of the "Objects" section, she or he is faced with explaining "A Frightful Release," "A Time to Eat," "In Between," "A
Little Called Pauline," "Suppose An Eyes," "It Was Black, Black
Took" as objects. The real challenge comes in the discrepancy between the neat list of titles at the beginning of "Food" and the
titles as they actually appear, in all their irrelevance and redun-
dancy, in the text itself.

Reading these subtitles carefully should be the final discouragement to interpretation: Stein's titles are no less playful and
freewheeling than her texts. The fragment called "Orange In" in
the text has its title listed as "Cocoa; and Clear Soup and Oranges
and Oat-Meal" in the initial list of subtitles of the "Food" section.
That phrase is the second line of the fragment, suggesting that

some of the subtitles were simply taken from the text after it was written, chosen for their independent merit as phrases rather than their aptness in labeling the fragment, or in naming its subject. The fragment called "Salmon," which reads in its entirety "It was a peculiar bin a bin fond in beside," immediately follows the line (from "Sauce") "Sauce sam in" (495). Evidently some of the subtitles were suggested randomly by other texts. Stein is playing, and playing entirely in the realm of language, without interest in representation of the material world. Presymbolic language *is* language-as-play, an alternative to the earnestness, the seriousness of symbolic language.

Having said that *Tender Buttons* cannot (or should not) be reassembled or interpreted in order to generate conventional coherence, one must reiterate that it does have significant articulations of lexical meaning, as does most of Stein's successful experimental writing. Confusion comes when the question of meaning is ensnared in the problem of representation, the troublesome connection between Stein's words and the object outside herself she focused on to generate them, her discussions of which have misled so many of her critics. Stein says she wrote *Tender Buttons* and the portraits of the period by focusing on her subject and writing down the words that emerged from her concentration, in what she calls a fusion of "outside and inside," or of the essence of the subject itself intertwined with her own experience of it.[12] Presumably, the structures and essence of the subject (an orange, a cloak, Mabel Dodge) are somehow preserved in the shape of the language. But given the uniformity of Stein's writing within any of her experimental styles, and the impossibility of deriving the subject of a piece from the writing itself without the clue of a title, the question of whether or not the subject is preserved in the shape of the language becomes irrelevant to the reader.

Rather than writing about them or even re-creating them, Stein used her subjects as relatively arbitrary focuses of the concentration which helped her enter the state of consciousness from which she wrote. To reach that state, one might concentrate on some feature of the world outside and, simultaneously, on a compatible point in one's own internal landscape: a mood, feeling, cluster of associations. One then lets language flow freely out of this double contact, but rejects whatever words seem inappropriate to it.[13] Concentrating simultaneously on an "outside" and an "inside" in this way seems to have the effect of cutting the language loose from coherence but not from meaning. The effort of maintaining that double concentration gives the language tension and energy. Focusing on single, compatible features of the external and internal terrain gives the writer a principle of selectivity which is necessary for the significant articulation of lexical meanings (the words chosen have some consonance). Conventional description is faithful to the external coherence of the object; free association and stream-of-consciousness are faithful to the internal coherence of consciousness, or the subconscious; and purely chance groupings of words ("word-salad") are faithful to no anterior coherence at all. This experimental writing, however, is neither faithful to an anterior (either external or internal) coherence nor completely random. It is, as we saw in "Portrait of Constance Fletcher," senseless and yet signifying.

As gestures toward content, the subtitles of *Tender Buttons* make as well as mock meaning. They divide the work, however arbitrarily, into sections, making it much more manageable, less intimidating, than it would be otherwise. They also give each fragment (again, however arbitrarily) a focus: the reader has something definite to hold constant (a box or an orange), almost as a back-board, against which the startling, fragmented images and words can bounce and return instead of flying off into ether. On the whole, "Objects" and "Food" are more successful than "Rooms" precisely because they are divided into short, titled fragments.

Similarly, words and phrases which are intelligible in relation either to the title of the fragment or to Stein's writing itself ("A sentence of a vagueness that is violence is authority and a mission and stumbling and also certainly also a prison" [*Tender Buttons*, 481]) appear sporadically within each fragment. They provide a temporary focus, which counterpoints the strictly incoherent bulk of the writing. The writing literally moves in and out of focus, and the focused work gives the unfocused an extra layer of resonance, as in this paragraph from "A Substance in a Cushion":

A cushion has that cover. Supposing you do not like to change, supposing it is very clean that there is no change in appearance, supposing that there is regularity and a costume is that any the worse than an oyster and an exchange. Come to season that is there any extreme use in feather and cotton. Is there not much more joy in a table and more chairs and very likely roundness and a place to put them. (*Tender Buttons*, 462)

"A Substance in a Cushion" is characteristic of *Tender Buttons* and of "lively words." It is anchored, quite literally, in the material world: filled with "substance" by the concrete nouns which, as we have seen, give the writing in this style solidity. Some, though only a small amount, of that substance is suggestive of cushions, or the materials and actions that make them: in the paragraph above, "a cushion has that cover"; "feather and cotton"; "chairs and very likely roundness and a place to put them." Elsewhere in the fragment: "A circle of fine card board and a chance to see a tassel"; "The disgrace is not in carelessness nor even in sewing it comes out out of the way;" "What is the sash like. The sash is not like anything mustard it is not like a same thing that has stripes, it is not even more hurt than that, it has a little top" (462–463).

These phrases make the writing at least partly about cushions, or a reference we might derive from cushions; perhaps they suggest the lush comfort and simple pleasure of the bourgeois domestic interior. However, precisely through such small relatedness to content, this writing demonstrates most clearly to what extent it is *not* about anything. If we read it honestly, without imposing on it our culturally inculcated demand for sense, order, and meaning, we see that the cushions and their sensory nexus are only a tiny part of the writing, hardly substantial enough to bear the responsibility of integrating it thematically. What we should notice about "A Substance in a Cushion" is not that it does indeed at times suggest cushions, but that most of the time it does not. The phrase "a substance in a cushion," for example, links the abstract noun "substance" with the concrete noun "cushion" in a richly polysemous way, but does not make an interpretable thematic point either about cushions or about substance.

How, then, do we read "A Substance in a Cushion," or the portraits, or *Tender Buttons*? We read them phrase by phrase, regis-
tering and appreciating as many of their possible meanings as we
care to. For "a substance in a cushion," a phrase typical of successful "lively words," the images and associations are limitlessly
pursuable. They all emerge from the juxtaposition of the firmness and grandeur of "substance" with the softness and triviality
of "cushion," a juxtaposition which suggests various partial, unresolved images of substantial cushions filled with numerous
varieties of cushion-filling substance. After "a substance in a
cushion" (title-as-text) there is another phrase, "The change of
color is likely," which again offers limitlessly pursuable connections of meaning: what changes color?; what does it mean for
such change to be "likely"?; leaves in autumn, fabric dyed, hair;
the list is endless. That phrase is connected to another, "and a difference a very little difference is prepared," which evokes a pano-
ply of tiny but carefully plotted differences. We read these
phrases just as we read "a substance in a cushion," and we read as
few or as many of them as we please.

But then how do we plough through the thirty-five pages of
Tender Buttons, or the hundreds of pages of portraits, of *GMP*, of
A Long Gay Book ? Is there any way of writing a critical account
of *Tender Buttons* that will be recognizable as such: that moves
through these specific, particular words — the writing contained
in *Tender Buttons* and no other — accounting for the importance
or significance of Stein having put them in this particular order,
under the title *Tender Buttons*?

I do not think there is any way of writing such a critical account of *Tender Buttons*, because I do not think it matters that
the work contains these particular words in this particular order.
Stein went beyond the book in this period. Though she did not
know it, she used the book as a reassuring convenience, not as an
operative structure. Phrase and then phrase, sentence and then
sentence ("the specific word next to the specific word next it chosen to be next it") are all we can know of this writing. Reading it
entails giving up altogether the idea of the book, of the coherent
work. We needn't plough through it at all. We need pay attention
only as long as the thrill lasts, the tantalizing pleasure of the

flood of meaning of which we cannot quite make sense. Criticism can describe how meaning functions in this writing, and what that kind of functioning means politically and culturally, but then it must leave the rest to the reader "who is not too busy"— the reader who seeks the liberating, anti-patriarchal experience of meaning that this "different language" affords.

In the late "lively words," the intermittent focus, which both helps and misleads us in the 1911–12 writing, is rare. The 1913 writing goes the furthest of the "lively words" in disrupting conventional word associations and activating the presymbolic, aural level of signification:

ORANGE

Why is a feel oyster an egg stir. Why is it orange centre.
A show at tick and loosen loosen it so to speak sat.
It was an extra leaker with a see spoon, it was an extra licker with a see spoon. (*Tender Buttons*, 495)

Pluridimensional or multivalent signification is available in this writing, but it is overshadowed by sound association. At times the conjunctions become forced and unnatural in this 1913 writing, rather than simply unfamiliar, as in "Eating":

It is so a noise to be is it a least remain to rest is it a so old say to be, is it a leading are been. . . . Eel us eel us with no no pea no pea cool, no pea cool cooler, no pea cooler with a land a land cost in, with a land cost in stretches. . . . Will leap beat, willie well all. The rest rest oxen occasion occasion to be so purred, so purred how. (*Tender Buttons*, 494)

Multivalent signification is sacrificed to the disruption of conventional language, just as incremental resonance was sacrificed to obsessive, mechanical repetition in the late "insistent" style. Mechanical repetition also mars the late "lively words," as in this sentence from "Orange In" (punning, appropriately, on "nuisance"):

A no, a no since, a no since when, a no since when since, a no since when since a no since when since, a no since, a no since when since, a

no since, a no, a no since a no since, a no since, a no since. (*Tender
Buttons*, 496)

There are, however, a few successful short pieces in the late
"lively words" style. They orchestrate sound and rhythm along
with (rather than instead of) meaning, in a tight overall structure.[14] The most successful of these is "Susie Asado," one of
Stein's best works in this or any style:

> Sweet sweet sweet sweet sweet tea.
> Susie Asado.
> Sweet sweet sweet sweet sweet tea.
> Susie Asado.
> Susie Asado which is a told tray sure.
> A lean on the shoe this means slips slips hers.
> When the ancient light grey is clean it is yellow,
> it is a silver seller.
> This is a please this is a please there are
> the saids to jelly. These are the wets these say
> the sets to leave a crown to Incy.
> Incy is short for incubus.
> A pot. A pot is a beginning of a rare bit
> of trees. Trees tremble, the old vats are in bobbles,
> bobbles which shade and shove and render clean,
> render clean must.
> Drink pups.
> Drink pups drink pups lease a sash hold, see
> it shine and a bobolink has pins. It shows a nail.
> What is a nail. A nail is unison.
> Sweet sweet sweet sweet sweet tea.[15]

Stein uses effectively the placement of words on the page for
variation of emphasis. The circular structure works as well here
as it does in "Rue de Rennes": the free play of Stein's writing prof-
its from such an underpinning. The prose surface of the piece is
startling but not so much so that meanings cannot penetrate it.
Its sounds and images are tightly unified. Almost all of the juxtapositions are successful "lively words": "told tray sure," "ancient
light grey," "silver seller," "rare bit of trees," "the old vats are in
bobbles," "lease a sash hold," and the wonderful "a bobolink has

pins." "Susie Asado" has the presymbolic playfulness, the anarchic richness of meaning, the sense of world-as-language redeemed from patriarchy as a miraculous, joyous plenitude, which characterize the best Stein.

The period from 1906 to 1913 was extremely productive for Stein, not so much in the number of great works she produced, but in the significance of the changes she wrought in language in the course of progressing, so steadily and rapidly, from the conventional writing of *The Good Anna* and *The Gentle Lena* to the radically experimental—pluridimensional, presymbolic, antipatriarchal—writing of *Tender Buttons* and "Susie Asado."

In 1914 Stein's writing changed. Shattered by the dislocations of World War I, and by its own extremity, it lost the brilliance of the best "lively words." But most of the elements of the experimental stylistic repertoire Stein had assembled by 1913 reappeared later, in various forms, in the comparatively long period between the wars.

CHAPTER 5

Voices and Plays

What a system in voices, what a system in voices. ("Pink Melon Joy," Geography and Plays, 356)

Stein begins to evolve an anti-patriarchal mode of dramatic writing in late 1913. The "lively words" begin to lose their energized density, their resonance; but the first voices since *Melanctha* speak in Stein's work, and she writes her first plays.

The 1913 plays ("What Happened," "A Curtain Raiser," and "White Wines" in *Geography and Plays;* "Old and Old" in *Operas and Plays*) are written in the "lively words" style, but they are more dramatic than the other works of 1913. "What Happened" and "White Wines" are dramatic on a technical level: they are divided into acts. "What Happened," Stein's first play, supposedly an abstract rendering of an event — the "essence of what happened"[1] — goes further in the direction of dramatic form. It is divided into speaking parts: "One," "Five," "Two." "White Wines" goes so far as to suggest action: its second "act" is called "House to House."

A more concerted attempt at dramatic form is also evident in these first plays. The writing is distinctly simpler, more patterned and conservative than the typical 1913 "lively words": quite possibly a concession to the demands of dramatic (as opposed to printed) literature in our time, when the ear can absorb so much less than the eye. Much of the writing in these plays is declarative: "Loud and no cataract. Not any nuisance is depressing."[2] "Hold hard in a decision about eyes. Hold the tongue in a sober value as to bunches."[3] These lines are readily speakable, and create a comic contrast between the absolute assurance of their tone and the indeterminacy and multiplicity of their meanings.

Gone are the tension and excitement from word to word that we saw in the best of *Tender Buttons* and in "Susie Asado," but there is a suggestion of dramatic progression, of movement through space and time, that the static, pictorial "lively words" did not have. The beginning of "White Wines," for example, can easily be read as a succession of distinct speeches, each echoing and modifying the one before:

> Cunning very cunning and cheap, at that rate a sale is a place to use type writing. Shall we go home.
> Cunning, cunning, quite cunning, a block a strange block is filled with choking.
> Not too cunning, not cunning enough for wit and a stroke and careless laughter, not cunning enough. (*Geography and Plays*, 210)

This is a variation on a theme in three voices, again comical in its earnest assertiveness. "Portrait of Constance Fletcher," "Susie Asado," and *Tender Buttons* contain no such progressions.

The issue of movement through space and time becomes more important in "A Curtain Raiser":

> Six.
> Twenty.
> > Outrageous.
> Late,
> Weak.
> > Forty.
> More in any wetness.
> Sixty three certainly.
> Five.
> Sixteen.

Seven.
Three.
More in orderly. Seventy-five.[4]

The words in this brief play are best seen as concrete localizations of abstract temporal and spatial positions, articulated in relation to one another and to an overall closed space-time. The play makes a "space of time filled with moving," the spatial-temporal paradigm that Stein says is typical of both America and the twentieth century.[5] It is also the spatial-temporal paradigm of drama, embodied (in a displaced way) in the unities of place and time. The space of the stage and the duration of the play are intertwined within a closed whole, a space-time. Each measures the other. Stage-time can be measured by movement through stage-space, and stage-space is a function of the stage-time each motion requires, since sets are designed to house configurations of action. Stage-time and -space are rigidly delineated, an image or embodiment of space-time. Any discrete segment of time can be seen as a space of time, but temporal-spatial discreteness is itself symbolically enacted in all drama, in the very existence of an acting area and a predetermined duration. Space-time is tangibly manifest in drama as in no other art.

The "space of time" of drama, also a "bright filled space" ("Plays," 71), is "filled always filled with moving" ("The Gradual Making of the Making of Americans," 98). Like the "space of time," the movement in Stein's drama is self-referential. Its specific form (speech, action) is secondary—localizing detail—which must only be lively enough to express the movement, and directionless or ritualized enough not to undermine the overall stasis. In this abstract vision of drama, the ideal play is the spectacle — the primitive religious ceremony,[6] the circus, the pantomime, the bullfight, vaudeville, and that "highbrow" spectacle, opera — or the dance, which is pure movement through space and time. In "Plays," Stein lists her inspirations as opera, circus, French drama (when she didn't understand the language), the bullfight, Isadora Duncan, and the Russian ballet. Avant-garde theatre has always drawn heavily on various forms of spectacle and dance.

In Stein's plays, as in all her experimental work, the real actors are words. The action is movement from one word or block of words, as localizations of space-time, to the next; and the stage is a metaphor for the arena of language as well as for space. In "A Curtain Raiser," each word locates a tone, a place, and a time within the play, making it dramatic without compromising its absolute abstractness. Numbers are perfect for such a task: they have no connotations or associations, and their primary functions are specifying and counting (moving from one to the next). The numbers are enlivened, in "A Curtain Raiser," by their alternation with more suggestive words such as "outrageous" and "wetness," each of which operates in a different way: "outrageous," like "certainly" and "weak," suggests a particular pitch and quality of voice; and "wetness," like "late" and again "weak," suggests a wide range of possible imagery and action. The repeated "more in" both refers to the sequence of numbers, which is generally increasing, and suggests various kinds of action.[7]

The clear movement through space and time comes in the ordering of the words on the page. There are innumerable ways to stage this play, but each should depend on the division into lines, the fixed sequence of numbers, the indentation of the words "Outrageous" and "Forty," the fact that "Seventy-five" is on the same line as "More in orderly." One might alter this configuration, but only deliberately, and only after first establishing it dramaturgically, much as a piece of music varies and alters its themes.

On the page, "A Curtain Raiser" looks like an abstract poem. But how meagre and dull it is as a poem, where numbers have no chance to realize their potential as pure distillations of space-time, and where linguistic texture is everything; how full of possibility it is, however, as a play.

In hindsight, we can see that Stein's discovery of drama, her first use of speech fragments or "voices," and the dissolution of her "lively words" — all coming in 1913 — are closely related, but she did not realize it at the time. The most conscious use of speech fragments and the clearest dissolution of the "lively words" can be found not in the plays of 1913, but in "Sacred Emily," the last piece listed in the *Yale Catalogue* for that year. At first, "Sacred Emily" seems to be much the same as "Susie Asado" and "Preciosilla," and is usually grouped with them, but it is really very different. Most of it sounds like the dense, tightly interconnected late "lively words," but there is a perfunctory quality in these lines which betrays the exhaustion of that style:

> Compose compose beds.
> Wives of great men rest tranquil.
> Come go stay philip philip.
> Egg be takers.
> Parts of place nuts.
> Suppose twenty for cent.
> It is rose in hen.
> Come one day.
> A firm terrible a firm terrible hindering, a firm
> hindering have a ray nor pin nor.
> Egg in places.
> Egg in few insists.
> In set a place.
> I am not missing.
> Who is a permit.
> I love honor and obey I do love honor and obey
> I do.
> Melancholy do lip sing.
> How old is he.
> Murmur pet murmur pet murmur.
> Push sea push sea push sea push sea push sea push
> sea push sea push sea.
> Sweet and good and kind to all.[8]

"Compose compose beds," "rose in hen," "firm terrible hindering," "ray nor pin nor," "egg in places" are all typical of the "lively words," but they are isolated, not part of a complex, energized, tightly woven texture of language. The division of these phrases into separate, end-stopped lines speaks of an invention goaded in fits and starts. Finally, after "Egg in few insists," the writing shifts to a mode immediately suggested by, and much better suited to, this succession of disconnected phrases: a montage of fragments of voices or speech ("I am not missing"). That line announces a new style — enter the speaker to claim her voice — just as surely

1111111111111111111111

as did "This has not any meaning" in "Portrait of Constance Fletcher."

The speech or voice fragments in "Sacred Emily," as in all the writing of this style (1914–19) — well over one hundred short pieces, most of them in *Painted Lace, Bee Time Vine, Geography and Plays,* and *As Fine As Melanctha* — are generally commonplace, banal, drawn from the vast stock of phrases used in superficial, everyday social and intimate conversation: "Leave us sit," "How do you do I forgive you everything and there is nothing to forgive," "Cordially yours," "I will give them to you tonight." Names, and other indications of conversation such as "Pause," begin to appear on the third page of "Sacred Emily": "Do you mind./Lizzie do you mind" (180). ("Sacred Emily" is also notable for the first appearance of "Rose is a rose is a rose is a rose," which later becomes "a rose is a rose is a rose is a rose.")

In a sense, these "voices" are diametrically opposite to the "lively words." While the "lively words" sought to dynamite conventional usage, this writing uses language in the most conventional way possible. These automatic phrases of politeness and endearment are in fact the definition of conventional language. It is precisely the automatic mindlessness of the speech fragments that the "lively words" are meant to eradicate.

But, in another sense, the two styles have a similar goal, which they share with the rest of Stein's experimental writing: the reinvention of literary signification. The "voices," in their very banality, are consummately anti-literary. They attempt to re-create and transcend the banal, mindless English of everyday speech by using that speech to achieve its affective opposite: a sense of mystery. The successful work in this style achieves that sense of rich mystery associated with the repressed anarchic underside of our straitened, everyday patriarchal vision; the unsuccessful work remains too closely connected to the trivial daily events that inspired it.

Unlike the subjects of *Tender Buttons* or the early portraits, the subjects of the 1914–19 work are often all too readily discernible: the irritations and privations of domestic life in wartime exile in Mallorca, details of household management, casual observations on the lives of Gertrude's and Alice's acquaintances, and intimate exchanges — defensive, sharp, teasing, loving — between the two women. In most of the 1914–15 monologues, only small ellipses separate this material in its raw form from what Stein offers as literature:

Everybody says something. Mike says that it is terrible the way the war does not finish. We know.

It was astonishing to find a sugar holder with the stars and stripes of liberty in an antiquity shop in Spain. I did it.

This is deeply felt. I wish I knew the English consul. He would be told. The american consul is not a consul he is a consular agent. That is different from a consul he cannot signify that there is a passport he can only receive it.[9]

Stein's impulse in this style is to dislocate the banal, and the patriarchal-hierarchical linearity on which the banal rests; to sever from its enveloping, normalizing factual context the discontinuous, irrational substratum of experience that surfaces in dream and fantasy. But simple ellipsis ("He would be told. . . . he cannot signify that there is a passport") has the effect of muffling this banal language, making it not less, but more trivial by concealing rather than uncovering its genuine resonance in the irrational.

The potential power of this language, as Beckett and Pinter know, lies in its domesticated familiarity: it is the last language we would expect to voice the absurd. When it succeeds, this writing shatters the convention of sane, cozy, comfortable, rational "real life" in which we ground our existence, by giving us a liberating glimpse of pre-Oedipal formlessness — redefined and repressed, by patriarchal order, as chaos. To do that, this homey language must prevent us from reconstituting through interpretation (filling in ellipsis) its reassuring sensibleness; it must disarm interpretation. In the passage from "I Have No Title to Be Successful," the coherence of the informing experience is only perfunctorily submerged, and a reader trained in interpretation will rest on a reconstitution of that experience as a statement, unsatisfying indeed, of what the writing is "about."

In the failed writing of "insistence" and "lively words," Stein went too far in eradicating meaning, using language to effect its own annihilation. In the failed "voices," Stein does not go far enough in the subversion of conventional meaning, the necessary basis of experimental writing. If this writing is not sufficiently de-defined, multiplied, and fragmented, it cannot be anything more than solipsistic records of daily trivia, interesting only as documents of Stein's domestic life.[10]

But, in a sense, the raw material of these "voices"—the snatches of everyday conversation and the kind of interior rambling known as "talking to oneself"—*already is* experimental writing. This language is at once the negation and the prime repository of absurd experience. Roland Barthes says as much in *The Pleasure of the Text*:

One evening, half asleep on a banquette in a bar, just for fun I tried to enumerate all the languages within earshot: music, conversations, the sounds of chairs, glasses, a whole stereophony of which a square in Tangiers (as described by Severo Sarduy) is the exemplary site. That too spoke within me, and this so-called "interior" speech was very like the noise of the square, like that amassing of minor voices coming to me from the outside: I myself was a public square, a *sook*; through me passed words, tiny syntagms, bits of formulae, and *no sentence formed*, as though that were the law of such a language. This speech, at once very cultural and very savage, was above all lexical, sporadic; it set up in me, through its apparent flow, a definitive discontinuity: this *non-sentence* was in no way something that could not have acceded to the sentence, that might have been *before* the sentence; it was: what is eternally, splendidly, *outside the sentence*.[11]

Stein's "voices" speak the fragmentary truth of life "outside the sentence." It is our penetration of our own cultural fictions of smoothness—penetration to the gaps, faults, craters beneath—that constitutes our experience of the absurd; again, there is the vertigo of dispensing with that monolithic illusion which has been necessary to the cultural life of patriarchy. That illusion or fiction of smoothness—the logical coherence of daily events—is so powerful that ellipsis does not dissolve it. As we have seen, dull coherence asserts itself in Stein's monologues through simple interpretive reading, what Jonathan Culler calls literary competence. Our everyday speech offers powerful resistance to its own unmasking.

Some of the 1914–15 monologues seem on first reading to baffle interpretation and to generate a sense of resonant, irrational dislocation or absurdity. But subsequent readings allow us to "make sense" of the writing, to fill in what prove to be only slightly larger ellipses:

Should you light it before the bridge. You mean before you come to the bridge. Should he light the light before he comes to the bridge. And if he strikes the match before he is seen to have seen the soldier should he be asked for his name and his house. He said he lived in a house. In a certain house. He was not angry. Not as angry as he was when the wind was blowing. You mean he has been. Yes. Very well then. Remind him.[12]

Two sentences in this paragraph seem at first to speak the casual, ominous, illogical logic of surrealism and the dream: "And if he strikes the match before he is seen to have seen the soldier should he be asked for his name and his house." "Not as angry as he was when the wind was blowing." As in the juxtapositions of "lively words," these sentences make no immediate sense, yet they resonate within a plausible consonance. The first sentence gives us an image of a match struck — perhaps to light a cigarette or the nebulous "light" of the title — in some way that arouses the interest or suspicion of a soldier who then asks for the "name" and the "house" of the lighter. An image of wartime curfew immediately forms, and the sense of mystery initially generated by the ellipsis disappears. Where the "lively words" juxtapositions ended with an irreducibly multivalent resonance, preventing unitary interpretation, the juxtapositions in the "voices" monologues are easily reduced to the thoughts or events which inspired them.

In "Not as angry as he was when the wind was blowing," we have an initially intriguing juxtaposition of anger and wind, simultaneously dissonant and consonant as in the successful "lively words." But in the context of the paragraph, we can see that "he" is the lighter of the light who has been accosted before by a soldier in the act of lighting, and was angry about it sometime in the past when the wind was blowing. Again, one feels a sense of deflation, disappointment upon arriving at this interpretation: not the "aha" one feels at deciphering a difficult passage in Eliot or Joyce, but rather a sort of "so what?" "Voices," perhaps more than any other Steinian style, reveal the inappropriateness of interpretation as a critical method for experimental writing, and the substantive difference between the complications of modernism and the radical subversions of experimentalism.

This writing does not require more baffling ellipsis—the emphasis should not be on such concealment—but rather an entirely different method of composition. In the monologues of 1914–15, Stein follows a fairly continuous train of private association, eliding information along the way. In the plays of 1915–17, Stein often achieves genuine dislocation, a revelation of the absurd substratum of daily life, by conducting many voices through the kind of dramatic progression in space-time that she discovered in the 1913 plays. Where the 1913 plays made abstract dramatic progressions of normally undramatic language, (from the "lively words" of "White Wines" and "Old and Old" to the radical reduction of "A Curtain Raiser"), the plays of 1915–17 explore the dramatic potential of the "voices."

In many of the plays of 1915–17 (almost all of them in *Geography and Plays*: "Ladies Voices," "Do Let Us Go Away," "For the Country Entirely," "Turkey Bones and Eating and We Liked It," "Every Afternoon," "Captain Walter Arnold," "Please Do Not Suffer," "Counting Her Dresses," "I Like It to Be a Play," "Not Sightly," "Bonne Annee," "Mexico") Stein achieves a deft comic counterpoint of speaking parts, not by differentiating them to reveal coherent character, as she did in *Three Lives*, but by using dramatic structure to play them off against one another:

(Theodore.) I don't think it's my fault I don't think I could do it so unconsciously. I think she brings it in every morning.
(Nicholas.) I used to be hurried, now I imagine I will not be.
(Theodore.) It is not necessary to dance or sing. Let us sing that song. Let us call them their names Nicholas. Theodore we will. We are dishonored. We visit one another and say good-bye.[13]

Reading this text gives us no desire to reconstitute its "real life" origins. It generates its own dramatic space-time, suggesting not coherent character or plausible action but voices pitched and paced in relation to one another, and sequences of "movement within a bright filled space." It is almost as if Stein is reinventing drama, beginning in 1913 with abstract movement through a closed space-time, then animating her stage two years later with the human voice, parcelled into speeches not only progressing from one to the next, as in the earlier plays, but responding to one another. It is this interplay of speech that makes drama drama, as Stein might say, and also makes "voices" successful experimental writing:

> Yes we do hear one another and yet what are
> called voices the best decision in telling of balls.
> Masked balls.
> Yes masked balls.
> ("Ladies Voices, A Curtain Raiser,"
> *Geography and Plays,* 204)

In dramatic "conversation" such as this the incoherent truth of life is most apparent. The fictive coherence which our patriarchal culture has defined as the norm is most palpably revealed as an illusion, a construct. By making plays rather than monologues of her speech fragments, Stein actually deconstructs, rather than attempts to conceal, the tenuous rational structures we weave of the fragmented things people say around us and to us, the things we say to them and to ourselves. The collections of words we might take as the prime instance of language as utterly transparent communication become instead the negation of coherent communication, the escape through the crevices of language, that is the foundation of experimental writing.

The dozen or so "voices" plays, most of them written in Paris in 1916 (the tedious monologues were largely the fruits of exile in Mallorca), vary greatly in the way they employ the speech fragments to make dramatic sequences. Many echo conventional dramatic form; some, like "Do Let Us Go Away," attach names to speaking parts; others use act and scene titles sporadically and incoherently, both to mock the convention, as did the titles in *Tender Buttons,* and to provide a kind of structural underlining:

Why do you make a noise.
Because we are isolated.
Have you not a watchman.
Certainly sir.

SCENE IV.

ACT IV.

First second third and fourth bird.
Do you like it.
All the time.[14]

In the last two plays of this period, "Counting Her Dresses,"
and "An Exercise In Analysis," of 1917, Stein predictably becomes
carried away by her game with formal subdivisions:

A PLAY

I have given up analysis.

Act II

Splendid profit.

Act III

I have paid my debt to humanity.

Act III

Hurry.[15]

But even a text as reduced and fragmented as this is capable of
generating interesting drama (in the imagination of a sympathetic stager). Like its more conservative predecessors, it is a
visually, kinetically suggestive, carefully paced succession of
voices, speaking to one another in plausible, startling comic in-
consequence.

In the final years of the war, when Stein and Toklas were in
southern France doing volunteer work for the American Fund for
French Wounded, Stein continued to write sequences of "voices,"
but they can no longer be called plays. Her writing in this period
is in tiny fragments, perfunctory and insubstantial, essentially no
more than evidence of her determination to go on writing no
matter what she produced. A typical piece in its entirety:

EXCEPTIONAL CONDUCT

We are exceptional.
Really exceptional conduct.
Can you please
If you please
In the likelihood that there is.[16]

It is not so much the brevity of this piece that differentiates it
from the plays of 1916. In effect, Stein has returned to the mode
of the 1914–15 monologues, breaking them up into short lines
and multiple voices instead of writing in first person continuous
narrative. In "Exceptional Conduct" and its contemporaries in
Bee Time Vine we see, even more instantaneously than we did in
"I Have No Title to Be Successful," or "He Didn't Light the Light,"
the inadequately concealed inspiration of the work, now more
often a passing sentiment than a recollected experience:

AMARYLLIS OR THE PRETTIEST OF LEGS

Thank you so much.
What can you say to shoes.
I don't like the leather.
What do you feel about the cut.
The sole looks pretty.
The sole looks pretty.
                    (*Bee Time Vine*, 196)

Interpretive reading, or literary competence, readily defeats the
ellipsis and repetition which, in addition to puns ("cut," "sole"),
barely complicate the pure transparence of this work.

A new difficulty, or perhaps one should call it an issue, arises
in this work. We can immediately see what these pieces are
"about," what their subjects are, and in the same instant we see
that those subjects are entirely trivial. Also, the writing has none
of the deranged resonance or activating dramatic structure of the
1916 plays. And yet there is an undeniable appeal in this writing,
in its very transparency, simplicity, self-effacing triviality. What
is the etiology of that simple, unostentatious appeal? How does it
affect what has emerged so far as the central sanction for experi-

mental writing: the simultaneous negation of coherent communication and retention of an interestingly fragmented, multiplied, skewed articulation of lexical meaning?

Marginal in the late "voices," whose simple appeal is also marginal, this difficulty or issue becomes central to Stein's work of the early 1920s.

CHAPTER 6

Melody

And this then began to bother me because perhaps I was getting drunk with melody . . . ("Portraits and Repetition," Lectures in America, *199)*

Stein's styles no longer progressed strictly chronologically in the twenties. Instead, she developed several styles concomitantly through most of the decade. Generally, however, "melody" dominated the early and late parts of the decade, and "landscape," the most important style after "lively words," dominated the middle.

The various forms of "melody" are the result of interesting but often fruitless experiments which Stein performed on the surface of language, primarily investigating the possibilities of writing as a form of music. Speaking of the early twenties in *The Autobiography of Alice B. Toklas*, Stein says "She also liked then to set a sentence for herself as a sort of tuning fork and metronome and then write to that time and tune."[1] (She also liked simply to sit in her beloved Ford car, Godiva, and listen to the street sounds, which "greatly influenced" her.) One of the first of the resulting poems is "Polish," 1920:

> Poling poling the sea into weather along.
> Poling poling dogs are pretty who have such a song.
> Girls and boys tease the seas.
> We are capable of this ease.
> Not so the Poles and their brothers the foals.
> They are the ones that made the Huns, do what.
> Be sick at their guns.[2]

Perhaps the organization on the page of the late "voices" fragments suggested the idea of poetry to Stein, and certainly it is the
idea of poetry as musical language she is pursuing here: the possibility of using poetry to engulf writing in patterns of sound.
Whether or not the reader can discover possibilities of meaning
in this work (Virgil Thomson says it is "about Poland and current
events") is finally irrelevant.[3] Whatever connections of meaning
there may be among the words are overwhelmed by connections
of sound and rhythm. Playfully, but arbitrarily, Stein is filling in
words to a preestablished "time and tune." As in the unsuccessful
late "insistence" and late "lively words," meaning is submerged
beneath the linguistic surface.

"Mary" is extreme but characteristic of 1920–21:

> Mary Minter and Mary P.
> Mary Mixer and Esther May.
> Henriette Gurney and Mrs. Green can you see what
>   I mean.[4]

"Mary" is unabashedly trivial, giving us only rather crude internal prosody and a singsong nursery meter. But nonetheless its
failure to offer meaning is less disturbing than the "senselessness"
of a work like *Tender Buttons,* where meaning is present but multiplied, deranged, shattered. Since meaning is clearly and simply
absent here, one needn't feel frustrated or inadequate at not being
able to find it, nor need one condemn the work for obscuring
something it never pretends to offer.

"Mary" is completely unresistant, transparent, pliable. These
qualities make it not only inoffensive but also, to some, appeal-
ing: it is easy, light, happy work by a notoriously "difficult"
writer. With the laughing bow and scrape of the court jester,

Stein seems voluntarily to renounce the power she acquired over the reader through the unsettling disruptions of her earlier work. These poems are often pleasing in a more conventionally sophisticated way as well: "Henriette Gurney and Mrs. Green can you see what I mean." Of course we cannot see what she means, or rather we can see that she means nothing. This type of joke is a variation of Stein's characteristic verbal dissonance: "the Poles and their brothers the foals," or this sequence from "A Hymn" of 1920:

> Indeed an account knows
> Which way they rub their woes
> And in the middle Christmas
> There is butter.[5]

Juxtapositions such as "account knows," "rub their woes," and "middle Christmas" might well be found in *Tender Buttons*, but submerged as they are here beneath the time and tune, they spark only a mild sense of comic incongruity rather than the powerful realignment of language and meaning they might effect in the "lively words" writing. Such comic incongruity, as in the "voices," appears at many levels in these poems: not only in individual juxtapositions and in a vocabulary ludicrously mixed of sophisticated and childish words, but also, and perhaps primarily, in the dissonance of the mock-serious, lecturing, assertive tone and syntax on one hand and the nursery rhyme sing-song on the other.

But beyond its absolute accessibility and its verbal wit, this work offers a more significant kind of pleasure as a primary, visceral, presymbolic language. As its nursery rhyme meter signifies, it returns us to the infant's state of linguistic experience, where all we absorb of language is sound and rhythm. As Julia Kristeva argues, the melodic and rhythmic patterns of our language form part of the intense, primal, undifferentiated sensation of infancy, when we are still merged in omnipotence with the outer world, with the "mother's body." The process of acquiring or entering patriarchal culture is concomitant with the gradual transformation of language as sound to language as sign. But that transformation represses, rather than destroys, our connection with the mother's body and with presymbolic language. The initial impact of language as internal/external sensory event, as melodic and rhythmic pattern, is submerged but not obliterated by the culturally ascendent language of the Father, which is exclusively a tool for ordering and communicating meaning.[6] The dominance of time and tune to the exclusion of meaning in Stein's early twenties writing allows us to reexperience, as a return to that intense sensation of infant pleasure, an alternative, nonpatriarchal state of language.

I dwell on the nature of the appeal in these minor poems because they represent an important option for experimental writing. Until the early twenties, writing of Stein's which failed to articulate meaning also failed to offer any sort of access to the reader, still less any interest or pleasure. Here is writing that offers both ready access and also a wholly different kind of pleasure, unrelated to the presence or absence of readable meaning (in some poems, such as "A Hymn" or "Polish," there are connections of meaning among the words; in others, such as "Mary," there are not).

The appeal of these poems also comes from the relief they provide both from the difficulty of Stein's other work and from the alienating difficulty of the increasingly complicated uses of symbolic language in twentieth-century writing. But most important, this writing represents the fullest possible liberation of Kristeva's repressed female *jouissance:* an assertion of the freed "magic of the signifier" (Barthes) over the repressed, hierarchical order of the signified.

However, it is difficult to attach such significance to the verse we have seen so far in this chapter, which seems to have been written mechanically, without the concentration, commitment, and powerfully original invention that characterize Stein's best work. These poems do not have sufficient force to restore to language, or restore language to, the magic of the signifier. Later in this chapter we will see a much less compromised, more successful form of melodic writing.

Not all of Stein's early twenties poetry submerges meaning entirely beneath the linguistic surface. Though time and tune still govern the composition in a work like "Sonnets That Please," meaning also functions in the text in an interesting way:

SONNETS THAT PLEASE

I see the luck
And the luck sees me I see the lucky one be lucky.
I see the love
And the love sees me
I see the lovely love be lovely.
I see the bystander stand by me. I see the bystander stand by inside me.
I see.

Another Sonnet That Pleases

Please be pleased with me.
Please be.
Please be all to me please please be.
Please be pleased with me. Please please me. Please please please with me please please be.[7]

These "sonnets" do not "please" through comic dissonance: they contain no incongruous juxtapositions, no mixed vocabulary, no mock-earnest assertion. Like the other 1920–21 poems they "please" through pure sound, but here the simple pleasure of time and tune is also reinforced by the simple pleasure of sentiment. Many conventional love lyrics, particularly in popular music, have little more content than these poems, and it is precisely the popular love lyric that Stein parodies here and at the same time emulates.

Both "Sonnets That Please" and popular love songs operate through an appeal to reflex sentiment. What any particular love lyric actually says is irrelevant to its effect: "I love how he loves me" calls up the same mass fantasy, with all its predictable ecstatic yearning, as "I'll be true to you" or "love me tender love me sweet," different as the contents of those statements seem. Stein draws her vocabulary in "Sonnets That Please" from the cliché horde of that popular fantasy, recognizing that all one needs in order to evoke the pleasurable reflex associated with the love lyric is any reasonable combination of words like "love" and "please," set to an appropriate time and tune.

Calling these pieces "sonnets" is not a reference to their prosody but rather, I would imagine, an announcement that they are intended as love poems. Stein's approach to genre here is characteristically abstract. Just as she wanted to make her first play "the essence of what happened,"[8] she is attempting in "Sonnets That Please" to render the essence of the love lyric. But while her abstract approach to plays yielded powerful dramatic forms, her abstract approach to the love lyric — a form the word "sonnet" would suggest she takes seriously — arrives only at its most banal component.

However, at the same time that they imitate the popular love lyric's appeal to automatic sentiment, the "Sonnets That Please" also parody the genre precisely by revealing the irrelevance of the coherent sense the conventional lyrics make. As far as emotional impact is concerned, "I love how he loves me" might just as well be "I see the lovely love be lovely." But there *is* a difference at the level of linguistic surface: the puns and other verbal play separate Stein's work from popular cliché and give it the appearance of a more sophisticated, or at least literary, kind of writing. That difference allows us to read "Sonnets That Please" as parody or verbal wit or pure musical language without sacrificing our enjoyment of the pat sentiment which is the strongest element of its appeal. That combination of formal invention and banal sentiment makes "Sonnets That Please," and Stein's other early twenties work like it, typical of a good deal of popular avant-garde literature and therefore inimical to the project of experimental writing, which is to provide culturally alternative modes of signification in literature, not to conceal pat, conventional themes beneath a deceptive surface of unconventional language.[9]

It is this kind of spurious experimentalism that allows Norman Holland, in *Dynamics of the Literary Response*, to claim that the appeal of *all* avant-garde or "difficult" art is only in the distraction or defense the unconventional form provides from the enjoyment of threatening or forbidden fantasy content.[10] According to Holland, when we think we are fitting together the fragments of an avant-garde work to organize it into a large thematic statement about modern life, what we are actually doing is distracting and defending ourselves from the knowledge that we're basking in forbidden sexuality. This argument is useful in its recognition that form and content can have wholly divergent impact, but it falsely discredits the formal preoccupations of avant-garde art by making the impact of form seem entirely subservient to the impact of the content. Again, Holland is able to make his argument categorical because there is a large class of avant-garde art in which the fragmented form does conceal or distract from, without complicating, fairly banal, straightforward, or conventional content — content which is often the raw sexual fantasy which Holland discovers in his analysis of contemporary film.

Stein's poetry of the late twenties and early thirties avoids banal content, but not banality. In her best known poem, "Before the Flowers of Friendship Faded Friendship Faded" of 1930, Stein employs for her metronome not the singsong of nursery rhyme but, entirely at the other end of the poetic spectrum, the free, largely iambic rhythms of serious modern poetry. In "Before the Flowers," and also in most of the book-length "Stanzas in Meditation" of 1932 (some of "Stanzas" is like "Polish" and "Mary"), Stein seems to be trying to capture the structural and emotional essence of poetry itself. Unfortunately, she seems to equate the essence of poetry with the way many poems sound, and instead of illuminating abstraction she achieves only travesty:

> In the one hundred small places of myself my youth,
> And myself in if it is the use of passion,
> In this in it and in the nights alone
> If in the next to night which is indeed not well
> I follow you without it having slept and went.
> Without pressure of a place with which to come un-
>   folded folds are a pressure and an abusive stain
> A head if uncovered can be as hot, as heated,
> to please to take a distance to make life,
> And if resisting, little, they have no thought,
> a little one which was a little which was as all as
> still,
> Or with or without fear or with it all, . . .[11]

"Before the Flowers" has an added liability: it was meant to be a translation of a fairly conventional poem by Georges Hugnet (Stein's title refers to the consequences of his reading her version). Much of the painfully unassimilated "poetic" diction in Stein's poem is the trace of the French original. "Stanzas in Meditation" is not as oddly interspersed with hackneyed, melodramatic language ("use of passion," "nights alone," "abusive stain"), but it too attempts to realize the essence of poetry by imitating, ingeniously enough, its rhythms and seriousness of tone:

> I have not heard from him but they ask more
> If with all which they merit with as well
> If it is not an ounce of which they measure
> He has increased in weight by losing two
> Namely they name as much.
> Often they are obliged as it is by their way
> Left more than they can add acknowledge
> Come with the person that they do attach
> They like neither best by them altogether
> For which it is no virtue fortune all
> Ours on account theirs with the best of all
> Made it be in no sense other than exchange
> By which they cause me to think the same
> In finally alighting where they may have at one time
> Made it best for themselves in their behalf.[12]

Though this verse, typical of the "Stanzas," does not have the pretentious patches which are the mark Hugnet left on "Before the Flowers," it does contain diction ("obliged," "acknowledge," "attach," "altogether," "virtue," "fortune," "alighting") which Stein had banished from her earlier experimental vocabulary as weak, abstract, or pompous. One can only assume that Stein considered such language a necessary concession to "serious" poetry.

Unlike "Polish" or "Mary," this work invites no return to a powerful presymbolic linguistic bliss. But like "Sonnets That Please," it is premised on an appeal to reflex reading, not through the mawkish fantasy of Romance but through the brooding seriousness of Poetry. Stein tries to put us in an elevated spiritual realm without doing the difficult work required to get us there.

The result, to this ear, is just plain silly. It is unlikely that Stein intends comic travesty in either "Before the Flowers" or "Stanzas." This work represents a genuine attempt to realize the essence of poetry, which fails because Stein is no longer in the safe, simple realm of popular cliché or fantasy. Her method is simply too superficial for the complex uses of language it attempts to assimilate.

It may seem impertinent to give these works, particularly "Stanzas in Meditation," such short shrift. Other readers have found and no doubt will continue to find in them qualities to value. However, we do not fail in respect for Stein by remaining faithful to our actual experience of reading her. If a work, however long it is or however substantial in the canon it appears, fails to offer anything to a reader, there is no point in pursuing a reluctant analysis.

There is an important exception — a mode of early twenties "melody" based entirely on rhythmic repetition of a few words:

A Very Valentine

Very fine is my valentine.
Very fine and very mine.
Very mine is my valentine very mine and very fine.
Very fine is my valentine and mine, very fine very
mine and mine is my valentine.[13]

This section of "A Valentine to Sherwood Anderson" is similar to "Sonnets That Please" in its poetic line structure and in its playful appeal to conventional sentiment. But not only is the repetition more concentrated here, the rhythm has a subtly different quality. While "Sonnets That Please" used the simple nursery rhythm that we saw in "Polish" and "Mary," the more complex rhythm of "A Very Valentine" is a function of the sounds of the words themselves as they are repeated and recombined rather than of an externally imposed, preestablished pattern.

In his book *Roots of Lyric*, Andrew Welsh makes a very useful distinction, mainly via Frye, Valéry, and Pound, between what he calls song-melos and charm-melos.[14] Charm-melos is related to Welsh's third root of poetic sound, speech-melos, in that both derive from sound and rhythm patterns internal to a language, while song-melos is an externally imposed musical pattern. Charm-melos is essentially a heightening or concentration of the natural, internal sound patterns of speech-melos. Together, these three roots form "melopoeia," which, along with Pound, Welsh distinguishes from "phanopoeia": "Phanopoeia in poetry drives toward precision of image and thought, the clear, precise seeing and knowing that is needed for a good riddle or a good Image poem. Melopoeia, on the other hand, is a force that leads poetry away from precisions of word and meaning, but that may be, as Pound said, a bridge to a non-verbal consciousness."[15] It is easy to recognize in this distinction the idea that Stein's experimental writing is an anti-patriarchal exploration of a literary language prior to, and cut loose from, coherent sense.

Within melopoeia, it is charm-melos that has been most overlooked by poetry:

New books of poems appear each year with the word "songs" on their title pages [song-melos], . . . Similarly, each generation of poets reaffirms the spoken language as a source of the rhythms of poetry [speech-melos] . . . The third root — less well recognized, perhaps, but no less fundamental — lies in the mysterious actions of the closed, internal rhythms of language, the echoing reflections of sound we have called charm-melos.[16]

It is in the dense sound patterns of charm-melos that Stein finds another powerful means of reinventing literary signification. As Welsh points out, charm-melos is primarily concerned with power, both in the primitive cultures where it originates and in the subsequent uses to which it has been put (Welsh gives examples from Shakespeare, Blake, Poe, Valéry, and Pound): "The language of the charms is a language of power, and that power comes primarily not from lexical meanings, archaic or colloquial, but from other meanings hidden deep in the sounds and rhythms."[17] Those "other meanings" are precisely what I have been calling presymbolic signification. Their power, so often called magic, is the power of experimental writing.

We are beginning to see how complex an effect the seemingly

very simple writing of "A Very Valentine" has. Unlike "Polish" and "Mary," "A Very Valentine" does not use the shortcut of childish rhythms to take us back to presymbolic language. By avoiding that shortcut, "Valentine" also avoids the negative connotation of the word "childish." The presymbolic language-state can be experienced as powerful magic — Barthes's "magic of the signifier" — which is where its value lies, rather than as regression to immaturity or infantilism — escape from the adult responsibility of making sense — which is where its danger lies; evidence "Polish" and "Mary."

Moreover, "A Very Valentine" demonstrates the close connection between language as music and language as incantation (Welsh considers incantation part of charm-melos). In "Valentine," in fact, it is difficult to differentiate the two, since both are a function of the repetition and recombination of the sounds of the words. But as we know from "insistence," it is quite possible for incantatory writing to be entirely unmusical, unmelodic. "Insistence" is musical only in its dependence on repetition in time. Its monotonous, droning sounds make no independent music; they merely support the incantation: "This thing that is such a thing, this thing that is existing, that is a frightening thing to one, is a way of living of very many being living . . ." ("Rue de Rennes," 349).

By combining incantation with melody, "A Very Valentine" weaves together two experimental modes which define separate language-states, each of which opposes, from a different direction, the ordering, dominating mode of patriarchal-symbolic, sense-making language. The two are more effective combined than either is alone.

Writing in the style of "A Very Valentine" functions powerfully at the level of lexical meaning as well. "A Very Valentine" itself does not, because it uses the same kind of appeal to reflex emotion that "Sonnets That Please" uses: no reiterative recombination of "fine," "mine" and "valentine," particularly under the title "A Valentine to Sherwood Anderson," could undermine the pat, sentimental impact of the initial statement "very fine is my valentine." But in other instances of this style, Stein avoids that problem:

Not only wool and woolen silk and silken not only silk and silken
wool and woolen not only wool and woolen silk and silken not only
silk and silken wool and woolen not only wool and woolen silk and
silken not only silk and silken not only wool and woolen not only
wool and woolen not only silk and silken not only silk and silken not
only wool and woolen.[18]

If I told him would he like it. Would he like it if I told him.
    Would he like it would Napoleon would Napoleon would would he
like it.
    If Napoleon if I told him if I told him if Napoleon. Would he like it
if I told him if I told him if Napoleon. Would he like it if Napoleon if
Napoleon if I told him. If I told him if Napoleon if Napoleon if I told
him. If I told him would he like it would he like it if I told him.[19]

Shutters shut and open so do queens. Shutters shut and shutters and
so shutters shut and shutters and so and so shutters and so shutters
shut and so shutters shut and shutters and so. And so shutters shut
and so and also. And also and so and so and also. ("If I Told Him. A
Completed Portrait of Picasso," 230)

    What becomes of meaning in these passages? On one level, it is
obliterated. Repetition this intense has the effect of cutting the
verbal signifier loose, entirely, from lexical meaning — no longer
merely submerging meaning beneath the linguistic surface, but
bringing about a radical transformation of the reader's experience of the signifier. Through relentless repetition, Stein reveals
the signifier in its utter arbitrariness, totally divorced from the
signified — shattering, as Derrida does in *Of Grammatology*, the
notion of an "organic" or "natural" or "necessary" connection between signifier and signified. Tellingly, children often play the
game of repeating a word or a name until it becomes entirely a
disembodied set of sounds. The function of this game is to reveal
the wonder of the signifier, the wonder of language: language is a
great power, which normally effaces itself as mere representation, tool, mediation of direct experience. Again, as with Stein's
poetry of the earlier twenties, we temporarily reacquire the presymbolic order of language. However, in this writing, we reacquire it not as reminiscence which coexists with our subsequent
knowledge of sense-making, but, in moments of vertigo, as re-

turn to the pure state itself, in which words simply have no lexical meaning. Unlike the unsuccessful writing in Stein's earlier styles, where meaning is lost beneath the linguistic surface, leaving nothing in its place to activate the text, this writing uses the obliteration of meaning to enhance its primary effect: the "mysterious actions of the closed, internal rhythms of language, the echoing reflections of sound" of Welsh's charm-melos, and the intense, primal sensation of presymbolic language.

Paradoxically, meaning is magnified as well as obliterated in this writing. Intense repetition can always obliterate meaning, but if the repeated words are chosen in a certain way, repetition can also — not simultaneously but alternatively — intensify meaning. In the passages quoted above, several facets of Stein's choice and ordering of words enable this intensification of meaning. First, the repetition is not uniform. As in "insistence," it involves slight variations; also, more than one (usually three or four) verbal element is repeated. If only one word were repeated, without variation in its form, obliteration of meaning would be an absolute, unmitigated effect, as it is in unsuccessful late "insistence."

Stein also generates that alternative effect of intensification of meaning by employing some of the techniques she used in the "lively words" style. In the above examples, she chooses words with visual or tactile strength ("wool and woolen, silk and silken"); or words which portray a vivid, simple action ("shutters shut and open"); or juxtapositions of bizarre suggestiveness ("so do queens"), and tantalizing near-intelligibility ("would [Picasso] like it if I told him [he was] Napoleon"). These techniques serve to fix the image, action, or idea in the reader's mind firmly enough so that repetition can emphasize rather than (or as well as) obliterate it. Obliteration and intensification of meaning oscillate for the reader: in separate readings, or sometimes in the course of a single reading, obliteration or intensification of meaning alternately emerges, becomes "visible," as the other disappears. This double effect of obliteration and expansion of meaning, coupled with the powerful presymbolic "magic" of charm-melos, makes this "melody" extremely effective. It becomes a mainstay of Stein's writing in the late twenties.

CHAPTER 7

Landscape

They the magpies may tell their story if they and you like or even if I like but stories are only stories but that they stay in the air is not a story but a landscape. ("Plays," Lectures in America, *129–130*)

With hindsight, we can see the late twenties and early thirties as a transitional period for Stein in which she reinvented for herself, "from scratch," some of the structures of literary order she had abandoned two decades earlier, a reinvention which produced the relatively conventional writing of the thirties and forties. But one would like to think that Stein's preoccupation in this period with issues of continuity and integration would be clear even without hindsight.

Her work in this period is more diverse than at any other time during her career. The "melody" of Chapter 6 is characteristic of the period, but Stein wrote concomitantly in many other modes. Individual works of the early and mid-twenties vary greatly in length. Many works are only a few pages, while *A Novel of Thank You*, of 1925, is two-hundred-and-fifty pages long. They are generally a mixture or composite of several styles, succeeding one another without connection or integration.

One of these styles, related to the "melody," is a parody of verbose pomposity, a kind of parody which has become a staple of contemporary comedy: "On the fifteenth of November we have been told that she will go either here or there and in company with some one who will attempt to be of aid in any difficulty that may be pronounced as at all likely to occur."[1] Stein's familiar butt in this work is the corruption of language through excessive use of passive voice, pompous Latinate diction, and pretentious wordiness. She effects this parody partly by mixing understandable sense with absolute senselessness. Following that decipherable first sentence of her portrait of T. S. Eliot, Stein writes "This in case that as usual there has been no cessation of the manner in which latterly it has all been as it might be repetition." Here is a similar sequence of sense and nonsense from "Talks to Saints or Stories of Saint Remy" of 1922:

He spoke pleasantly indeed humourously, he described not each thing but several things and every one being pleased and excited they expressed their emotions freely. In this way nothing was changed except the illumination, that of course used to be other than it is.[2]

The two first sentences, though they omit concrete referents, make sense; the second sentences do not. The omission of concrete reference is parodic in itself, pointing up the intimate connection between pompous verbosity and vagueness (in effect Stein turns her penchant for undetermined reference, which she used for serious ends in her "insistent" writing, satirically against itself). Beyond that, the juxtaposition of a sentence which makes sense with a very similar sentence which makes none whatever reveals how close this pompous, verbose writing *always is* to senselessness. Stein's writing here is, simply, "doubletalk": a revelation of elaborate wordiness as an evasion of communication, an escape from the rigors of making sense. Unlike most of her experimental writing, which renounces sense, this doubletalk pretends to make sense, offering, as nonsatirical circumlocution does, highly abstract language as a spurious sign of profundity. The purpose of satirical doubletalk is precisely to expose and ridicule this spuriousness.

At the same time, the satirical doubletalk, like the early twenties poetry, makes no demands on the reader. We see immediately what it is; we know immediately how to respond to it. Like "Polish" or "Mary," if offers straightforward comedy; and even more accessibly, because it exists within one of the oldest, most firmly established comic conventions, it offers mockery and deflation of pretentiousness.

The central importance of this mode is the ability it gives Stein to "go on," as Beckett might say. The length of works such as *A Novel of Thank You* attests to this ability. This writing requires no concentrated, sustained creative energy. Quite the contrary: it is in the nature of wordiness to "go on," phrase attaching itself effortlessly to phrase, in the manner of Orwell's prefabricated hen house.[3] In renouncing the ordered successivity of linear writing, Stein had forfeited the almost automatic continuity available to conventional narrative: the steady propulsion through the text which we normally take for granted in reading. To retrieve in some form this continuity, without returning to conventional coherence, Stein built on the automatic "going on" of her satirically verbose pseudo-sense. She dropped the pretentious diction, concentrating instead the deceptive *appearance* of sense this double-talk generates by its use of standard syntax in conjunction with undetermined reference:

He said that they had meant to be there and they were not there and they had believed that they had been asked to be very careful about it. Every once in a while they might be there and just as soon as they instinctively withdrew they were very much more careful than they ever had been. That makes him every once in a while obliged to be as well. They knew that they cared about it every two months. Nearly every two months.[4]

With punctuation and specifying reference added, this writing might easily make conventional sense. In this respect, it is structurally similar to early "lively words" ("If they move in the shoe there is everything to do. They do not move in the shoe"). But the focus of the "lively words" was the irreducibly multiple, vivid juxtaposition, such as "move in the shoe." The deceptive conventional syntax was primarily connective tissue, increasingly omitted as the resonant juxtapositions, the "lively words" themselves, were concentrated. In the mid-twenties writing, which hovers much closer to sense than the early "lively words," it is the "going on" — the continuous movement of the writing provided by conventional syntax — that interests Stein. The vocabulary is of minimal interest, its primary purpose, I would imagine, to insure the incoherence threatened by the conventional syntax.

Writing such as the above passage from *A Novel of Thank You* is interesting primarily as a stage in the development of Stein's experimental writing, and as an abstraction of the principle of narrative continuity. Stein built on this principle of pure narrative movement to create an interesting and largely successful mode of writing: "landscape."

In her essays, Stein makes much of the idea of pure movement, or intensity of movement, as the core of her literary work. In "Portraits and Repetition" (*Lectures in America*), she generalizes this notion of pure movement to a defining principle of the "modern composition": "We in this period have not lived in remembering, we have living in moving being necessarily so intense that existing is indeed something . . ." (182). Hence it is "intensity of movement," not recognizable personality, that Stein attempts to render in her portraits: "I had to find out inside every one what was in them that was intrinsically exciting and I had to find out not by what they said not by what they did not by how much or how little they resembled any other one but I had to find it out by the intensity of movement that there was inside in any one of them" (183).

In "Poetry and Grammar" (*Lectures in America*), she connects the idea of "intensity of movement" to the peculiarly Steinian idea of a difference in "balance" between sentences and paragraphs:

Sentences and paragraphs. Sentences are not emotional but
paragraphs are. . . . When I wrote the Making of Americans I tried to
break down this essential combination by making enormously long
sentences that would be as long as the longest paragraph and so to see
if there was really and truly this essential difference between
paragraphs and sentences, if one went far enough with this thing with
making the sentences long enough to be as long as any paragraph and

so producing in them the balance of a paragraph not a balance of a
sentence, because of course the balance of a paragraph is not the same
balance as the balance of a sentence. (223)

That bizarre, provocative, categorical closing statement about
sentences and paragraphs is a characteristic Steinian formulation: condensed, penetrating, logically elegant, highly abstract,
excising the heart of very complex matters, yet deceptively
whimsical and simple in expression. To a certain extent, it is possible to translate this remarkable formulation into more conventional, perhaps more credible (though certainly less pleasurable)
terms.

   Stein felt herself to be pitted against both the sentence and the
paragraph throughout her experimental career. The sentence
would represent for Stein the conventional, hierarchical grammar and syntax which she had variously decomposed and de-
nied. The field of syntactical grammar, the ultimate referent of all
sense-making activity, is the sentence. And if the sentence is the
vehicle, the enforcer, of the language of the Father, the paragraph
seems to appear to Stein as the carrier of the larger, more complex units which sentences accrete to form: the coherent meanings, the thematic syntheses, which we value, in phallogocentric
culture, beyond anything else literature offers. The word "emotion" is generally pejorative for Stein. In *Narration* she associates
the "emotion" of the paragraph with "beginning middle and ending," or story, which she consistently repudiates for twentieth-
century literature.[5] In *The Autobiography of Alice B. Toklas*, she
describes her achievement as a writer as the "destruction of associational emotion" (211).

   It is not surprising, therefore, that she calls her narrative task
an attempt "to break down this essential combination" of the sentence and the paragraph. However, just as Stein wants to rescue
in narrative the continuous movement of "going on," she also
wants to rescue the combination, or fusion, of "intellectual" and
"emotional" elements — the smaller units of independent meaning
and the larger units of cumulative significance — that the sentences and paragraphs of conventional writing appear to her to
provide. Building on the continuous movement she achieved in

her pseudo-sense, which allowed her to retrieve continuity without abandoning incoherence, she uses the abstract notion of combining the "unemotional" sentence with the "emotional" paragraph to create a *significant* movement in her narrative — movement which does not merely exist for its own sake, but rather gives the sense of generating an accretion of meaning — without returning to conventional thematic coherence. As Stein puts it, she wants to create a "new balance" by combining the "unemotional balance" of the sentence with the "emotional balance" of the paragraph: to retain the literary values the sentence and paragraph provide without returning to conventional forms. This "new balance" is generated for Stein precisely by intense movement:

I did in some sentences in The Making of Americans succeed in doing this thing in creating a balance that was neither the balance of a sentence nor the balance of a paragraph . . . my sentences . . . had no longer the balance of sentences because they were not the parts of a paragraph nor were they a paragraph but they had made in so far as they had come to be so long and with the balance of their own that they had they had become something that was a whole thing and in so being they had a balance which was the balance of a space completely *not filled but created by something moving* as moving is not as moving should be. ("Poetry and Grammar," 224–225, italics added)

Stein cites examples from *How to Write* of what she considers successful examples, "even in a short sentence," of this ideal "combination":[6]

> He looks like a young man grown old. (25)
> It looks like a garden but he had hurt himself by
> accident. (26)
> A dog which you have never had before has sighed. (27)
> Once when they were nearly ready they had ordered
> it to close. (29)
> If a sound is made which grows louder and then stops
> how many times may it be repeated. (89)
> Battles are named because there have been hills which

> have made a hill in a battle. (89)
> A bay and hills hills are surrounded by having
> their distance very near. (89)
>
> ("Poetry and Grammar," 226)

Stein employs a variety of stylistic devices in these sentences. The first is a paradox; the second, third, and fifth are non sequiturs; the fourth employs undetermined reference; the sixth is circular; the seventh is elliptical and abstract. But beyond that, each sentence gives the impression of what we might nonrigorously describe as covering a lot of ground. We get glimpses, hints, suggestions of intriguing, larger territories of meaning, which we must create ourselves; of "emotional paragraphs" implied and carried, but not elaborated, by these strictly "unemotional sentences." This impression is achieved, precisely as Stein claims, by the quality of movement each sentence contains: a leap from premise to illogical but suggestive conclusion in the non sequiturs; a telescoping of time in the paradox "he looks like a young man grown old"; a blurred or confused time sequence in the sentence of ambiguous reference; a sudden abortion of sequentiality, which "brings us up short," in the circular sentence; a surreal montage or rapid series of unresolved spatial relations in the landscape of bay and hills.

These sentences are *tours de force:* self-conscious sentence-paragraphs or paragraph-sentences. But they are also characteristic of Stein's best narrative writing in the late twenties, in which the movement is not only continuous, but also interesting, in that it imparts to the writing, by means of various leaps and foreshortenings, a sense of opening onto half-glimpsed territories of meaning which the reader is then responsible for imagining more fully:

It is true that at that time it was almost better to have loved and lost it. That made them be this as much as they could to think very well of it. It is very funny that it is not interesting to know what she said and to ask to always ask to always hear and to know what did she say then. That makes plenty of time for a photographer to talk about food.[7]

Something it was "almost better to have loved and lost" *is transformed into* something "they" thought "very well of" once "that made them be this as much as they could." People, an experience, a lost valued object. As in "lively words," the possibilities of meaning are tantalizingly, irreducibly multiple, up to the reader to generate; as in "insistence," Stein weaves together the specific and the general. But here the resulting configurations of meaning are continually shifting. They are neither pictorially static, as in "lively words," nor repetitiously incremental, as in "insistence." This writing is premised instead on the principle of narrative movement, of "going on." The "it" of the second sentence is related but not identical to the "it" of the first. The third sentence begins with an entirely different "it," shifting our attention to "what she said," and then to the related but different "what did she say then." Knowing and asking about "what she said" somehow "makes plenty of time for a photographer to talk about food": again the playful surprise and the irreducibly multiple, vivid meaning of "lively words," but here experienced in a context of continuous, significant narrative movement.

This work represents an effort on Stein's part to reinvent continuity and accreted significance in narrative without resorting to conventional coherence. At the same time that she was pursuing this exploration, which generated a good deal of successful writing, she was also moving in an opposite and much less fruitful direction, investigating the possibilities of establishing in writing the absolute integrity of the single word, thereby obliterating continuity altogether.

In the early twenties, Stein had begun to play with series of punning permutations: "Opium den opium then opium when"[8] or "Out from the holes Rosenberg, / Out from the whole Rosenberg."[9] Stein seems literally to be using the method of scientific experimentation here to investigate the force of the single word. With *How to Write*, first published in 1931, Stein's interest in the force of the single word becomes central. The ideal "sentence-paragraphs" which Stein quotes, from *How to Write*, in "Poetry and Grammar," are not typical of that work. It is dominated, in fact, by the opposite motive of restoring to the single word the integrity it loses in assimilation to the sentence. In conventional

linear writing, language is a smooth surface along which we glide
easily from one thought to the next, each word submerging its individual identity in the larger identity of the phrase, clause, sentence, which in turn become indistinguishable from what they
communicate. We have seen Stein attempting to restore continuity without restoring that transparency. But at the same time, she
was pursuing the literally opposite goal of destroying continuity
utterly by writing one word at a time, in such a way that it is virtually impossible for the reader to move from word to word.
Stein goes so far in this mode that she writes whole pieces with
periods between every few words: *They Must. Be Wedded. To
Their Wife.* is the title of a 1931 play.

"Arthur A Grammar" of 1928 begins "Successions of words are
so agreeable," then proceeds to make precisely that: successions,
rather than connections, of single, separate words:

Fire plans do rather exercise individually make left to temper never
call rely matter this in a call to be meant share that it is a relative
make in out of sound out of sound. . . . Upper half to make much
have a seemingly bewailing out included march plain carry account in
rope for the not which rested alike. Remember it just. Wire is it.[10]

It is easy to recognize Chomsky's ungrammatical "third degree of
grammaticalness" ("a the ago," "perform compel"), or utter aban-
donment of meaning, in this writing. These "successions of
words" are anything but "agreeable"; they are painfully difficult
to read. One word simply does not follow another. In the interest
of reclaiming the integrity of the individual word as an ultimate
form of the integrity of language — of restoring to words within a
sentence their separateness from the words near which they hap-
pen temporarily to be placed — Stein violates the sanction of all
literature that the reader have some way to move from one word
to the next. The prevention of reading is, of necessity, the denial
of literature. This writing offers nothing but the attempt to work
out a polemical idea of language. Though all of Stein's radical
work is frequently read as such, mere illustration of theory is
actually a limitation of only her least successful writing. Stein's
experiments in the integrity of the single word go as far as any of

her work toward the complete, and therefore sterile, triumph of the purity of language.

This sterile writing is not restricted to *How to Write*. It appears sporadically throughout Stein's work of the late twenties and early thirties. However, most of Stein's writing of the period is in other modes. The typical work of the mid-twenties is a composite of unconnected fragments of poetry, "melodic" repetition (such as "shutters shut" and "If I told him"), punning permutation, pseudo-sense, and sentence-paragraphs. These composite works have no overall unity or integration, no cohesion (as opposed to coherence). That is not, in itself, a criticism of an experimental work. But Stein's discovery of narrative continuity in the twenties engenders *for her* a turn or return to unity (integration, cohesion) as a literary value.

She effects that return by means of the recurring motif, a device which she used with great success in *Three Lives* ("Anna led an arduous and troubled life," "Lena was patient, gentle, sweet and german"). In the twenties writing, the recurring motif begins not as an abstraction of character, as it was in *Three Lives*, but as an abstraction of the principle of cohesion itself, just as the pseudo-sense functions as an abstraction of "going on." Stein uses her recurring motifs in the simplest possible way in the mid-twenties: by repeating a phrase throughout a work — playing with it in various constructions and as various parts of speech — she weaves a unifying thread through an otherwise disparate work. The motif of a work might disappear temporarily but it always returns.

The recurring motif first appears in the mid-twenties writing in utterly arbitrary relation to the rest of the text it occupies, as in "A Description of the Fifteenth of November. A Portrait of T.S. Eliot" of 1924:

On the fifteenth of November in place of what was undoubtedly a reason for finding and in this way the best was found to be white or black and as the best was found to be nearly as much so as was added. To be pleased with the result.

I think I was.

On the fifteenth of November have it a year.

On the fifteenth of November they returned too sweet. On the fifteenth of November also.

The fifteenth of November at best has for its use more than enough to-day. It can also be mentioned that the sixteenth and any one can see furniture and further and further than that. The idea is that as for a very good reason anything can be chosen the choice is the choice is included. (*Portraits and Prayers*, 68)

"The fifteenth of November" vanishes for a page and a half, but it returns:

On the fifteenth of November in increase and in increases, it increases it as it has been carefully considered. He has a son and a daughter and in this case it is important because although in itself a pleasure it can be a pleasure. (*Portraits and Prayers*, 70)

The motif returns again for a paragraph a page later, and makes its last appearance on the top of the last page. (The piece ends with the "not only wool and woolen silk and silken" passage discussed in Chapter 6.)

We have no sense in this writing that Stein considers the meaning of the phrase "the fifteenth of November" more than sporadically or superficially ("It can also be mentioned that the sixteenth") in her use of it as an integrating element. Again, the recurring motif is utterly arbitrary.

That changes quickly. The last work listed in the *Yale Catalogue* for 1925, immediately following *A Novel of Thank You*, is a seventy-five page piece called "Natural Phenomena." As in "A Description of the Fifteenth of November," Stein titles the work with the recurring motif which integrates it. But unlike "the fifteenth of November," the phrase "natural phenomena" integrates the work more than superficially — so much so that we might call it a theme:

Lists of Natural Phenomena.
Thunder winter and lightning lakes, borders and feathers, shawls hangings and traceries birds hours and at once.
These make phenomena of nature steadily even more steadily they make phenomena of nature steadily. They make phenomena of nature steadily.[11]

References to nature, independent of the phrase "natural phenomena," also appear throughout the work:

Would it be very certain that rain and its equivalent sun and its
equivalent a hill and its equivalent and flowers and their equivalent
have been heard and seen and felt and followed and more around and
rounder and roundly. Is there also a hesitation in going slower. She
said yes. (174)

This work, in its structure as well as its content, inaugurates
Stein's preoccupation in the late twenties with what she calls
"landscape." Her choice of the word "landscape" arises from her
involvement with the Rhône valley country around Belley, where
she and Toklas began to spend their summers in this period, and
also, of course, from her intimate acquaintance with landscape
painting. But the literary principle of "landscape" has less to do
with landscape painting, or with the quality of the Rhône valley
countryside, than with Stein's notion of intensity of movement as
the central interest in genuine twentieth-century writing. For
Stein, the "American thing" — which is the same for her as saying
the "modern thing" or the "important thing" — is to create an integrated, simultaneous, static whole which is made up of continuously moving parts. Stein contrasts this dynamic model to the
linear movement of the "English" nineteenth century:

Another thing you have to remember is that each period of time not
only has its contemporary quality, but it has a time-sense. Things
move more quickly, slowly, or differently, from one generation to
another. Take the Nineteenth Century. The Nineteenth Century was
roughly the Englishman's Century. And their method, as they
themselves, in their worst moments, speak of it, is that of "muddling
through." They begin at one end and hope to come out at the other:
their grammar, parts of speech, methods of talk, go with this fashion.
The United States began a different phase when, after the Civil War,
they discovered and created out of their inner need . . . the Twentieth
Century. The United States, instead of having the feeling of beginning
at one end and ending at another, had the conception of assembling
the whole thing out of its parts, the whole thing which made the
Twentieth Century productive.[12]

In "Plays," in *Lectures in America*, she first formulates this model of the twentieth-century dynamic, ascribing it to her plays, as "bright filled space" (112), then as "silence stillness and quick movement" (116), and finally as "landscape," the primary feature of which is that "it is there." Speaking of *Four Saints in Three Acts*, she says:

it made a landscape and the movement in it was like a movement in and out with which anybody looking on can keep in time. I also wanted it to have the movement of nuns very busy and in continuous movement but placid as a landscape has to be because after all the life in a convent is the life of a landscape, it may look excited a landscape does sometimes look excited but its quality is that a landscape if it ever did go away would have to go away to stay.
Anyway the play as I see it is exciting and it moves but it also stays and that is as I said in the beginning might be what a play should do. ("Plays," 131)

Along with its paradoxical dynamic of overall stasis and constant constituent motion — "it moves but it also stays" — the other crucial feature of "landscape," related to its static element, is its unity. A landscape is an integrated whole, all its parts existing, as Stein says, "in relation, one thing to the other:"

The landscape has its formation and as after all a play has to have formation and be in relation one thing to the other thing and as the story is not the thing as any one is always telling something then the landscape not moving but being always in relation, the trees to the hills the hills to the fields the trees to each other any piece of it to any sky and then any detail to any other detail, the story is only of importance if you like to tell or like to hear a story but the relation is there anyway.[13]

Though her discussion here is limited to plays, her formulation of "landscape" applies equally well to her prose narratives of this period (as she says in "Plays," "I slowly came to feel that since the landscape was the thing, I had tried to write it down in Lucy Church Amiably and I did . . ."[122]).

With "landscape," Stein adds cohesion or unity to the conventional literary values (continuity, cumulative significance) which she had already re-espoused. She does so in the late twenties without, as yet, re-espousing conventional coherence or sense, the despised "story": "Everybody knows so many stories and what is the use of telling another story" ("Plays," 118). Despite this repudiation of "story," and though Stein continued throughout the rest of her life to write experimentally, her "landscapes" do mark the beginning of a return to conventional, or at least conventionally interpretable, writing. With the exception of the late novels *Brewsie and Willie* and *The World is Round,* the conventionally written works of the thirties and forties are either essays or memoirs. The latter spring from the famous *Autobiography of Alice B. Toklas* of 1932, the crucial structural origins of which lie outside Stein's experimentalism. Like *Three Lives, The Autobiography* is in many ways characteristically modernist, with its impressionistic or associative temporal structure, following the course of memory rather than chronology. Its compelling voice is that of Stein's reported conversation: wry, whimsical, a peculiar mix of understatement and exaggeration. It is this voice, coupled with Stein's free-ranging memory of historically interesting personalities and events, which are the core of *The Autobiography.*

But the memoirs are the exception. Stein's other writing of the thirties and forties, though almost never as *radically* experimental as her earlier work, is still experimental. In essence, it is the same as the various "landscape" modes of the late twenties. The case is clearest for the operas and plays and for the fiction, which, though fairly coherent, are still manifestly experimental (*Ida, Mrs. Reynolds,* the late works in *Last Operas and Plays*). The connection to the earlier work of the thirties essays, many of which are written as conventionally as Stein ever writes, is not as apparent. However, the clarity of essays such as those in *Lectures in America* is primarily due to their having originally been, as the title announces, lectures. Structurally, they are similar to a kind of "landscape" writing which we might call "meditation," borrowing from the unfortunate "Stanzas."

Stein's first meditation is also her first relatively coherent lecture-essay: "Composition as Explanation," delivered at Cambridge and Oxford in 1926. This essay is structured around a few motifs or keywords, similar to the motifs of "A Description of the Fifteenth of November" and of "Natural Phenomena," except in this case the motifs are abstract ("composition," "time-sense," "beauty," "classic," "beginning again," "continuous present"). Moreover, they are explained; that is, the entire essay is devoted to exploring and, to some extent, communicating the meaning of the motifs. That is the difference between the relatively conventional critical essays, including "Composition as Explanation," and the strictly experimental meditations of the late twenties and early thirties (most of them in *How to Write*), where communication of coherent meaning is not a value. But all these meditations are structurally similar; they revolve around a cluster of abstract motifs or keywords, each of which Stein takes up, elaborates from various angles, drops temporarily, then takes up again, just as she does with "natural phenomena" and even "the fifteenth of November."

This similarity in structure is clearest in the least conventional of Stein's later meditations, *The Geographical History of America* of 1935. Here Stein plays freely with the abstract keywords that absorbed her at the time (primarily "human nature" and "the human mind," but also "memory," "geography," "resemblance," "play," "writing," "events," "superstition," "money," "propaganda," "because and become," "romanticism," "masterpieces"). She jostles these notions against one another and records the results, which are repetitive, arbitrary, frequently unconvincing but also frequently profound. Again, this work resembles the late-twenties "landscapes" much more closely than it does a conventionally written essay.

With the *Lectures in America* the resemblance is not as clear: since they *are* lectures, they are less repetitive and more lucid than the freely written *Geographical History*. But they too are organized around key motifs, which, like the emblematic keywords of *Three Lives*, seem arbitrary and opaque at first but accumulate large significance through the series of intellectual contexts Stein creates around them. When we first read in "What is English Literature," for example, that "daily island living" is entirely responsible for that great body of writing, we are sceptical.

But as Stein takes us through the centuries of English literature, exploring for herself and for us what she might mean by that, we gradually become delighted, and perhaps even convinced, by the powerful, fresh crystallization this unlikely notion generates.

The original, experimental meditations of *How to Write* can make no such claim to profundity, or even to the cumulative significance of the few sentence-paragraphs they contain. In fact, most of them are heavily interspersed with the unreadable successions of single words. But they also contain suggestive articulations of their titular motifs or keywords. In "Arthur A Grammar" of 1928, instances of the "third degree of grammaticalness" alternate with such articulations:

> Forget accountably raining this is do make a fanned it looking best love to be similar to face it the does mellow matter to them business of course.
> Hopping in at all conspicuous in a trained horn.
> Grammar is the same as relative.
> Grand in well tell how means and mast.
> Grammar felt in telling that not telling in stories.
> Can be angry that with all he did not need to care need care careful apple appear justifiable capable. Grammatical whimsies one two cured fruit.
> Why do some things that are darned in medicament pensively demanded.
> Grammar is drained with by and to. (49)

Grammar is at issue throughout this passage, when it is violently abrogated as well as when it is obliquely but significantly discussed. It is no coincidence that the "third degree of grammaticalness," the extremest possible violation of grammar, cohabits these pieces with resentful but fascinated meditations on sentences, paragraphs, narrative vocabulary, "forensics," and grammar itself. As in her sentence-paragraphs, Stein is grappling directly with the forms of conventional writing which she had freely disrupted or avoided for so long.

It is important to remember that Stein's commitment in the late twenties and early thirties to continuity, cohesion and cumulative significance is not itself continuous, cohesive, or cumulative.

As we have seen in the successions of single words, she continued
to write concomitantly in modes that took her as far experimentally as she ever went. Such extreme works appear even among
the "landscapes." One of these is a lengthy piece called "Patriarchal Poetry,"[14] written early in 1927, whose title is extremely suggestive to a feminist reader.[15] However, in all but one respect, the
title-motif of this piece generally bears as arbitrary a relation to
the rest of the text as that of "Description of the Fifteenth of November." Most of "Patriarchal Poetry" not only defies interpretation, it defies reading.[16] In fact, Wendy Steiner's pejorative phrase
"militantly unintelligible" is an apt epithet for this extreme example of experimental writing as destruction of literature. Though
the phrase "patriarchal poetry" is a consistently recurring motif,
its characteristic appearance is in passages such as the following:

Patriarchal Poetry net in it pleases. Patriarchal Poetry surplus if rather
admittedly in repercussion instance and glance separating letting
dwindling be in knife to be which is not wound wound entirely as
white wool white will white change white see white settle white
understand white in the way white be lighten lighten let letting bear
this neatly nearly made in vain. (290)

Here is another characteristic passage, which continues in the
same vein for another twelve lines:

Once threes letting two sees letting two three threes letting it be after
these two these threes can be two near threes in threes twos letting
two in two twos slower twos choose twos threes never came twos two
twos relieve threes twos threes. (255)

Though this writing is reminiscent of the melodic repetition of
"wool and woolen silk and silken" or "shutters shut and open," it
has none of their crucial charm-melos. Stein builds no reiterative, incantatory rhythm, no complex patterns of sound with
these repetitions; because she shifts the rhythm so frequently, the
writing reaches us as blank tedium. As in the successions of single
words of *How to Write*, Stein's movement toward continuity, integration and cumulative significance generates a simultaneous
desire to destroy those qualities: a desire which is probably both

an expression of ambivalence or resistance and also a reflection of the dialectic turn of her mind.

Just as she calls her utterly ungrammatical writing by the name of what it repudiates (many of the pieces in *How to Write* have the word "grammar" in their titles, and if not "grammar" then something like "Saving the Sentence"), she titles "Patriarchal Poetry" with the name of what its writing demolishes: sense, coherence, lucidity, hierarchical order (she mockingly capitalizes the phrase throughout the piece). Hence, though there is little *interpretable* feminist thematic content in this work, its feminist, or at least *anti*-patriarchal implications, whether or not Stein intended them, are profound.[17]

In 1927, the year inaugurated by "Patriarchal Poetry," Stein wrote (or began) two of her most important experimental works: *Four Saints in Three Acts* and *Lucy Church Amiably.* The merit of both works has been greatly disputed, opinions ranging from Sutherland's encomia (calling *Four Saints* the greatest drama in English since Shakespeare,[18] and *Lucy Church* the "purest and best pastoral romance we have had in this century,"[19]) to Bridgman's dismissals ("*Four Saints in Three Acts* occupies a more important position in Gertrude Stein's canon than its intrinsic worth can justify."[20] "She [Stein] correctly observed that 'Lucy Church made mountains out of mole hills.'[21] Her prose is rarely less banal than that example. . . . When Gertrude Stein rises to sustained comprehensibility, the information communicated is of little moment"[22]).

Both works are characteristic and largely well realized examples of Stein's "landscape." But satisfying as they are, their central importance comes not so much from their merit as individual works, but rather from their role in Stein's *oeuvre*. They determine the shape of Stein's lasting return to the conventional genres of prose narrative and drama. (After 1927, Stein's work falls rather neatly into conventional genres; and after the failures of "Stanzas in Meditation" and "Before the Flowers of Friendship Faded," those genres consist almost entirely of operas and plays, prose narratives or "novels," memoirs, and essays or meditations.) Of the genres which *Four Saints* and *Lucy Church* initiate, the dramatic mode proved to be the more fruitful and important for Stein. Thus, though *Four Saints* comes first chronologically, I will reserve it for last.

Lucy Church Amiably, begun late in 1927 and not completed, according to Bridgman,[23] until 1930, is the first full-length narrative of a kind which Stein began writing earlier in that year. We have already seen one example of it: "Felicity in Moonlight. A Traveler's Story" (*Painted Lace*, 64–66). That work is not a fully realized "landscape" narrative. But, like them, it has continuity and cumulative significance. All it lacks as "landscape" is the integration or unity provided by a recurring motif. Stein had already composed a very short but largely cohesive "landscape" narrative by that time: "Duchesse de Rohan. A Writer." After a brief opening paragraph concerning "how to compare Iceland and three Poles in a wood," the rest of the piece is clearly integrated by the Duchess of Rohan:

> The Duchesse de Rohan was very sweet very responsive and very nice.
> She was not different from either or or a memory or a description or to an extent. This is why one thing at once a frenchwoman can be very nearly come to be able to come to-day. Rousseau and she she was describing having mentioned the number a convent he was describing having mentioned the number a place where they had had their day.
> The Duchess of Rohan was a woman who wrote poetry with a rhyming dictionary but that is very well. Poetry consists in a rhyming dictionary and things seen. The Duchess of Rohan is a poet. Not having forgotten any one can remember and this is very well this is all very well.
> And now I leave Mr. Paul to tell it truly. How I heard how we heard how he heard how she heard.
> Thank you.
> Madame de Rohan's poetry is determinate and interesting. (*Painted Lace*, 310)

Bridgman's condemnation of *Lucy Church Amiably*—that the "information communicated," even when it "rises to sustained comprehensibility," is "of little moment," could well apply to "The Duchesse de Rohan." Stein is still in her radically experimental period, and she simply is not interested in communicating information. To the extent that this fragment has value, that value lies not in what we learn about the Duchess of Rohan or about poetry, but in the experimental pleasure of such sentence-paragraphs as "Rousseau and she she was describing having mentioned the number a convent he was describing having mentioned the number a place where they had had their day." Such writing gives the pleasure of continuous, cumulative, but mysterious and unresolved movement through half-glimpsed territories of meaning, a movement which confers on us the privilege of imagining these territories for ourselves.

In *Lucy Church Amiably*, Stein realizes this mode of "landscape" narrative more fully than she does in the earlier fragments of 1927, not so much by means of an externally imposed recurring motif, though "Lucy Church" functions as such, but by means of a genuine thematic center. But it is important to remember, nonetheless, that a loose, general thematic preoccupation is not the same as interpretable thematic coherence. *Lucy Church Amiably* allows no thematic synthesis, develops no argument, no Gombrichean "illusion." It evolves no coherent patterns of meaning, it imposes no clarifying order. As Bridgman says, most of it is, by the standards of conventional literary expectation, banal, irrelevant, incomprehensible. But though *Lucy Church Amiably* has no coherence, it is constructed around an identifiable, consistent set of feelings, values, attitudes, preoccupations. Bridgman makes this claim for thematic center in almost all of Stein's work. I would argue that only in this period of transition to more conventional modes of writing does her work become thematically centered.

As we have seen, Stein begins to re-espouse other conventional literary values in this period as well. As a mode of writing, "landscape" is premised precisely on this re-espousal of continuity and cohesion, without concomitant return to clarity, order, coherence. Therefore, we can take experimental incoherence as assumed, and claim that the more powerful the mode of cohesion in a piece of "landscape" writing, the more successful that writing is. Thematic center is a powerful mode of cohesion.

The characteristic thematic center — the unity of meaning — in the "landscape" writing is an elaboration of the recurring motif or proto-theme of "Natural Phenomena." In Stein's best "landscape" writing, particularly *Lucy Church Amiably* and *Four Saints*, the content or thematic center is in sympathy with the structural principles of the writing, not in the feeble sense of form imitating content, but in the sense that both arise from and express the same essential vision. It is a new vision for Stein, a new serenity: an active and energetic but unperturbed, untroubled sense of union with the natural world, perfectly reflected in the structural unity or integration, and the peaceful stasis comprised of constant energetic motion, of the "landscape" writing. The natural world includes, for Stein, the human, and this inclusion is most easily effected in a natural landscape (or, as we will see, among saints), where purely human manifestations do not overwhelm. *Lucy Church Amiably* is "about" nature, and human beings as part of nature, not looking at it, but as Stein says, "sitting in it": "To bring them back to an appreciation of natural beauty or the beauty of nature hills valleys fields and birds. They will say it is beautiful but will they sit in it."[24] In *Lucy Church Amiably*, Stein attempts to make us all "sit in it": to draw us inside the circle.

Critics have had no trouble recognizing this vision of beatific harmony in *Four Saints*, but it has eluded them in *Lucy Church*. They are misled by Stein's own "Advertisement" of it as "a novel of romantic beauty and nature":

a return to romantic nature that is it makes a landscape look like an engraving in which there are some people, after all if they are to be seen there they feel as pretty as they look and this makes it have a river a gorge an inundation and a remarkable meadowed mass which is whatever they use not to feed but to bed cows. ("Advertisement," *Lucy Church Amiably*)

Though Sutherland sees that the "ease of relationship between the human and the natural elements of the composition" that Stein arrives at in this period "brought her very naturally to her novel of romantic nature, *Lucy Church Amiably*,"[25] he says later that the novel is about the "easy and delicate pleasure of life," comparing it to Picasso's twenties neo-romanticism: "even Picasso in these years was indulging in agreeable subject matter and quite often in large easy lines as never before."[26] Though Sutherland praises the novel highly, this characterization is in essential agreement with Bridgman's dismissal of its triviality: ". . . lackadaisical as a vacation . . . a leisurely summer book."[27]

The words "pretty" and "engraving" in Stein's own "Advertisement" foster this misreading. We might more profitably dwell on her announcement of a "*return* to romantic nature," "romantic" not in the sense of sentimentality or triviality but in the sense, usually capitalized, of the great early-nineteenth-century movement, which espoused the same kind of saving union with nature that Stein proposes here. The tone, the emotion of Stein's "romantic nature" are very different from Wordsworth's or Keats's: she has none of their complex ambivalence, their rapture, or their exquisite despair, but rather a quiet, lively sense of achieved, playful, painless, utterly "natural" union. However, her project is similar to theirs in sincerity and scope, as well as in ultimate aim.

Sutherland describes the "kind of existence expressed" in Stein's "landscape" writing as "intimately involved with the existence, growth and movement of things in the landscape," a "sense of continuity between human life and the life of the world."[28] It is no coincidence, I would argue, that the subject of the particular passage he discusses here is a woman. Stein's version of a "return to romantic nature" reflects a conscious articulation of what has been one underlying force behind her experimental writing throughout: the anti-patriarchal, pre-Oedipal continuity with the mother's body, as representative of the natural, physical world (world of things), that constitutes in patriarchy the repressed female mode. Again, this pre-Oedipal continuity with the mother's body, the world of things, is the one feature of anti-patriarchal experimental writing that is explicitly female, because it is directly of the province of the Mother. Before the "landscape" writing, this explicitly female mode realized itself in Stein's work as the presymbolic writing of the dominant signifier, as in late "lively words" and in "melody." With "landscape," it comes to be articulated as thematic content.

It has long been held in Western culture that continuity or

union of self with the body and the processes of nature is the special province of the female. Historically, this belief has been a cornerstone of patriarchal mythology, relegating woman to the "lower," material sphere, trapping her in the generative body, confirming her unfitness for the "higher" life of intellect and spirit. But feminists both here and in France are currently reclaiming nature and the body for a positive version of female culture.[29] Like them, though without their conscious political intent, Stein destroys this Western hierarchical dichotomy of mind and body, spirit and nature in her late-twenties writing, substituting for it a polymorphous continuity or union. And it is precisely this union, this reintegration, this abolition of "higher" and "lower," that Kristeva claims female culture, as the embodiment of what Western phallogocentrism represses, can achieve for all of us.

Internal evidence points to a shift in Stein's feeling toward femaleness in this period which might have some bearing on this new thematic explicitness of the long-present female impulse. Her sexual identity had been a terrible problem for her early in life. Essentially, she connected her self-hatred, insecurity, fearful dependency, passivity, and inertia, to her female gender. This is evident in several of her early writings, particularly in *Fernhurst* of 1904–05, written just before she met Alice Toklas:

The young woman of to-day up to the age of twenty one leads the same life as does her brother. She has a free athletic childhood and later goes to college and learns latin science and the higher mathematics. She in these days busies herself with sport and becomes famous on the ball-fields . . . as if there were no sex and mankind made all alike and traditional differences mere variations of dress and contour.

I have seen college women years after graduation still embodying the type and accepting the standard of college girls — who were protected all their days from the struggles of the larger world and lived and died with the intellectual furniture obtained at their college — persisting to the end in their belief that their power was as a man's — and divested of superficial latin and cricket what was their standard but that of an ancient finishing school with courses in classics and liberty replacing the accomplishments of a lady. Much the same as a man's work if you like before he becomes a man but how much different from a man's work when manhood has once been attained.

. . . .

There is a dean presiding over the college of Fernhurst in the state of New Jersey [based on M. Carey Thomas of Bryn Mawr] who in common with most of her generation believes wholly in this essential sameness of sex . . . I have heard many graduates of this institution proclaim this doctrine of equality, with a mental reservation in favor of female superiority, mistaking quick intelligence and acquired knowledge for practical efficiency and a cultured appreciation for vital capacity and who valued more highly the talent of knowing about culture than the power of creating the prosperity of a nation.

. . . .

Had I been bred in the last generation full of hope and unattainable desires I too would have declared that men and women are born equal but being of this generation with the college and professions open to me and able to learn that the other man is really stronger I say I will have none of it. And you shall have none of it says my reader tired of this posing, I don't say no I can only hope that I am one of those rare women that should since I find in my heart that I needs must.[30]

Informing this passage are disillusion, bitterness, regret, self-deprecation, and ultimately confusion. It weaves together Stein's conflicting identifications with powerless women who delude themselves and with powerful men who know better. She is "the young woman of to-day" who is made to feel equal to, or at least no different from, "her brother" (no doubt Leo) "up to the age of twenty one," but who discovers after that age what other women do not: that her "power" is not "as a man's." However, in pointing out the folly of her feminist contemporaries, Stein separates herself from them, and by implication aligns herself with men: like men, she lives in the "real" world and possesses its wisdom. But, since she is a woman, her power is *not* as a man's, and her dubious advantage over other women is that she knows it. As a woman, she resents the education which both misleads her about her equality with men and denies her that equality. The constructive anger that might emerge from her resentment is thwarted by her simultaneous identification with men, through which she scorns women and hence herself. She is paralyzed, divided against herself in an all-too-familiar way. Her male identification, which makes her feel strong like her oppressive father, tells her that women are inferior by nature rather than circumstance.

Her inevitable self-deprecation is clear in her remark about women who mistakenly value "more highly the talent of knowing about culture than the power of creating the prosperity of a nation." Here she denigrates her own ability and predilection, which she sees as female, and wistfully admires the "male" business talents of someone like her father. She can have power only as a man, which means only at the expense of repudiating both her femaleness and her talent. As long as she must remain female, she is not only paralyzed but condemned to hate herself. All the sad, self-defeating irony of her position is contained in the phrase, "the *other man* is really stronger"; and the contradiction at the center of her sexual self-image, which generates the irony of that phrase, results in the confusion of the last sentence: "And you shall have none of it says my reader tired of this posing, I don't say no I can only hope that I am one of those rare women that should since I find in my heart that I needs must." What is this "posing"? She doesn't "say no" to what? She "should" what? She "needs must" what? But ambiguous as Stein's referents are in that sentence, her turmoil is clear.

With Alice Toklas as her wife and Pablo Picasso as her peer, Stein was able to live fully the male identification which allowed her to accept herself. Once Picasso became her "role model," which her book about him indicates he was, she need no longer equate the "talent of knowing about culture" with inferior femaleness. Also, the fact that she was Baby needn't undermine her power as long as Mama was also subservient wife rather than dominant father or brother. Once her liaison with Toklas was established, Stein made the following remark in her notes: "Pablo & Matisse have a maleness that belongs to genius. Moi aussi, perhaps."[31] To summarize the argument once more, in a Steinian struggle for full expression at the expense of repetitiveness: because her self-hatred was connected to being a woman, she could not relinquish the idea that women were inferior, incapable of great things. To do great things she must be a man.[32]

That Stein's disparagement of women is connected to self-hatred, and her male identification to self-assertion, should be clear in her notorious advocacy of the crackpot gender theories of turn-of-the-century Viennese psychologist/suicide Otto Weininger. In his book *Sex and Character* he makes women hopelessly passive idiots and assigns all available energy and intellect to men. Crucially, he adjusts his theory to fit "exceptions" like Sappho, George Sand, and George Eliot by granting them an invigorating dose of "maleness" and noting that the sign in women of a moiety of maleness is lesbian sexuality.

Stein clung tenaciously to her redeeming "maleness" as long as public rejection of her writing reinforced the depression, insecurity and self-hatred that she equated with her gender. When, in the twenties, she finally acquired a substantial audience, and attitudes toward women in the arts improved, those feelings began to change. By the time she wrote *The Geographical History of America* (1935), she was able to say, several times, that the "only literary thinking in this century was done by a woman." Here she is clearly able to integrate her idea of herself as a genius with her idea of herself as a woman: precisely the two aspects of self which had been mutually exclusive. Shortly after that, in *What Are Master-pieces*, came the even larger remark that "what women say is truer than what men say." In other words, women are closer to the heart of truth, otherwise called by Stein the "human mind" or "god," than men. This position is in a sense a full reversal of her earlier Weininger-influenced equation of "maleness" with "genius." Finally, in the year of her death, 1946, she wrote *The Mother of Us All*, an opera libretto wholly sympathetic to its heroine, Susan B. Anthony.

This shift in sexual self-image toward greater acceptance of her gender may have fostered or enabled the female vision of *Four Saints* and *Lucy Church Amiably*. The latter book is not only centered thematically in the female vision of positive continuity with nature; it is also replete with female images and subjects: all forms of flowing water, particularly waterfalls; the "widening," horizontal movement of simultaneity — "right to left and left to right" as Stein says — "richness" or plenitude; kinship relations; "amiability" itself (one thinks of Jane Austen). The characters in the novel have highly indistinct "ego boundaries," a female trait identified by Freud which we are only now learning to see in a positive light. Instead of rigid delineation, Stein's characters have what we can now call protean, continuously shifting, composite identities, which dissolve the absolute distinction not only of gender (two of the characters are named John Mary and Simon Therese), but also of the human and the nonhuman: the heroine, Lucy Church, is part woman and part building (the peculiar church in the hamlet of Lucey which has a pagoda for a steeple), as well as part Stein and part Toklas.

Of course, though there are characters and a thematic center in *Lucy Church Amiably,* there is no story, no illusion-building, no conventional coherence. The thematic material is both fragmented and static, making regular but unpredictable and undeveloped appearances among the sentence-paragraphs which dictate the actual experience of reading the text: mysterious movement through half-glimpsed territories of meaning, the "movement in and out, continuous but placid" of Stein's "landscape" writing. The bulk of the book's "content" is comprised of deranged elements of conventional narrative—family relations, observations, quotidian events of private life—always colored by Stein's central thematic concerns:

Lucy Church made witnesses witness an inundation of the river
Rhone. There has been nothing mentioned about it because usually it
happens and very often they know that tributaries as is usual as is
usual as is peaceful as is peaceful as is happily as is happily they are
how many are there now present after there has been every effort
made to gather them together. (193)

These defining features of *Lucy Church Amiably*—its shifting, loosely drawn characters, its "continuous but placid" movement through deranged, fragmented narrative space, embodying a vision of life as unordered, unresolved process (rather than nineteenth-century "story" with "beginning, middle and ending") —continue to shape Stein's narrative writing in the thirties and forties. Though her later novels, particularly *Brewsie and Willie* and *The World is Round,* contain much more conventional, coherent narrative sequences than *Lucy Church* does, just as the lecture-essays of the thirties are far more lucid and accessible than the meditations in *How to Write*, they originate equally clearly in this twenties "landscape" work:

What happened one winter evening, the snow was falling and the snow was very white. While it was very white, there was no light. While Angel Harper is forty-nine, said Mrs. Reynolds there never is any light, that is in the street, and it must not shine out. But anyway whatever Mrs. Reynolds had to say, it was snowing and the snow was white and there was a light. Well it was moonlight and it was so light that Mrs. Reynolds said what is the use of there not being any light, and she was right there is no use in there not being any light.[33]

As in *Lucy Church Amiably*, this writing is open, freely constructed, nonlinear, "using everything" as Stein says in "Composition as Explanation." But at the same time it is continuous, significant, cohesive, integrated by its central thematic concerns.

Lucy Church Amiably is successful landscape writing, but as Stein herself says, her plays are even more so:

Then I began to spend my summers in Bilignin in the department of the Ain and there I lived in a landscape that made itself its own landscape. I slowly came to feel that since the landscape was the thing, I had tried to write it down in *Lucy Church Amiably* and I did but I wanted it even more really, in short I found that since the landscape was the thing, a play was a thing and I went on writing plays a great many plays, ("Plays," 122)

The misquote of Hamlet is deliberate: Stein sees a play quite literally as "a thing," and therein lies its superior suitability as "landscape" writing: the materiality of theatre matches that of actual landscape, and materiality is at the heart of Stein's vision of the continuity of human intellect and spirit with the natural world.

The materiality of Steinian drama is the "landscape" materiality of the spectacle. Stein acknowledges her debt and affinity to the circus, the bullfight, and that highbrow spectacle, opera. Both landscape and spectacle are "just there," or static, as Stein says in "Plays"; both are "bright filled space," both contain constant movement but tell no story. The "continuous but placid" movement of Steinian landscape drama, entirely different from the steady narrative continuity of *Lucy Church Amiably*, is essentially similar to the abstract movement through theatrical space-time of the "voices" plays. That movement was achieved by means of successions of abstract dramatic speech, pitched and paced in relation to one another (see for example *Ladies' Voices* or *A Curtain Raiser*). In "landscape" drama, Stein substitutes for sequences of speech sequences of writing in various styles, adapting the composite structure of early twenties works such as "A Valentine to Sherwood Anderson," which were essentially series of fragments in unrelated modes (various forms of "melody," pseudo-sense, successions of single words, etc.). The movement from style to style in a successful work like *Four Saints* is so smooth that the writing seems harmonious; it is surprising and various, but not the patchwork of disjoint styles that characterized the earlier work. Like the movement of nuns as Stein describes it in "Plays," the movement from style to style in *Four Saints* is "busy" and "excited" but "placid":

ACT ONE

Saint Therese in a storm at Avila there can be
rain and warm snow and warm that is the water is warm
the river is not warm the sun is not warm and if to
stay to cry. If to stay to if to stay if having to
stay to if having to stay if to cry to stay if to cry
stay to cry to stay.
Saint Therese half in and half out of doors . . .
Saint Therese silent. They were never beset.
Come one come one.
No saint to remember to remember. No saint to remember.
Saint Therese knowing young and told.
If it were possible to kill five thousand chinamen
by pressing a button would it be done.
Saint Therese not interested.[34]

The "melodic" modes of the early twenties are crucial here, not only for the manifest reason that words written according to sound associations are ideal words to be sung, but also because they provide an extreme contrast to the more coherent modes of articulating meaning that dominate the writing. This contrast enhances both the "excited" quality of the continuous movement, and also, paradoxically, the overall stasis of the work (the "melodic" writing itself is intensely static).

Successful as it is, *Four Saints* is certainly improved by appropriate music. I think Richard Bridgman goes too far in claiming that the libretto of *Four Saints* has no independent merit whatsoever.[35] But I do think Virgil Thomson's music adds immeasurably to the work (Thomson commissioned the libretto and initially set it to music exactly as written, even though Stein freely granted him permission to cut and rearrange). The music and the libretto are sympathetic in both structure and content, in form and in feeling. The fact that both employ religious themes is only the most evident similarity. (Thomson uses various snatches of American church music.) Everett Helm's description of the score in *Music Review* could be applied verbatim to the writing: "The seemingly naive score is in fact extremely skillful and sophisticated. The harmonies are essentially simple, even primitive; the ways in which they are manipulated, however, are refined—the rhythmic procedures no less so."[36] Like the writing, Thomson's music shifts continually, like a kaleidoscope turning, from fragment to unresolved fragment, mode to mode: a paradigm of the continuous movement within overall stasis of "landscape." As a musical friend of mine says, it "rocks back and forth between cadences that go nowhere," creating a "constant brightness" (this friend was unaware of Stein's formulation of the "bright filled space").[37]

Thomson's music helps the writing not only because it suits perfectly, but also simply because it is music. Theatrical production helps in a similar way. As John McCaffrey says in his article on Steinian drama "Any of Mine Without Music To Help Them":

And, of course, there are numerous plays by Gertrude Stein waiting to be done "without music to help them" [a phrase of Stein's]. What is needed is a director who can orchestrate the voices of his actors, activating that world in the silences around Stein's words with the life that the better music has discovered there.[38]

In fact, as we have seen, the "silences around Stein's words" are only silent, except in the unsuccessful work, to the unadventurous reader. Her writing is replete with potential, multiple, unresolved meaning: meaning not to be unearthed and ordered as in conventionally "difficult" writing, but to be recognized and at the same time invented by the reader. Music and staging "help" by suggesting, clarifying, embodying the dimensions of those noisy, teeming "silences."

Even without the notion of "landscape," it would no longer be necessary to argue for the thematic integrity of *Four Saints*. All critics of the opera recognize at its center the union of the spirit and nature — of all life — which we have seen in *Lucy Church Amiably*. In fact, the theme is both clearer and more pervasive in the opera then in the novel. But *Four Saints* was written, or at least finished, earlier than *Lucy Church Amiably*, and whether or not chronology is to blame, this union does not have the painless, untroubled, achieved quality in *Four Saints* that it has in *Lucy Church*. In fact, it appears in the opera as conflict or antithesis in the process of being resolved. The paradox inherent in "landscape" as a literary mode dominates *Four Saints*, while its ultimate harmony dominates *Lucy Church*. That paradox lies in the opposition of "excited," "busy" continuous movement with overall stasis, harmony, "placidity," and the parallel opposition of troubled immanence and serene transcendence. Saints enact for Stein both the paradox and its resolution, both antithesis and synthesis, just as Lucy Church, simultaneously human and inanimate, "sitting in" the landscape, enacts the untroubled harmony of *Lucy Church Amiably*.

In "Plays" Stein says of *Four Saints*, "I made the saints the landscape." Saints, as actual human beings who are nonetheless eternal, transcendent spiritual entities, are an ideal embodiment of Stein's dissolution and reintegration of the classical Western dichotomies. Saints can be said always to have enacted for our tragically gender-divided culture the potential unity of mortal and divine, immanent and transcendent, flesh and spirit. Stein's explanation of how St. Teresa became "actual" to her is a wonderful example of her sense of the continuity of the mundane and the transcendent:

As it happened there is on the Boulevard Raspail a place where they make photographs that have always held my attention. They take a photograph of a young girl dressed in the costume of her ordinary life and little by little in successive photographs they change it into a nun. These photographs are small and the thing takes four or five changes but at the end it is a nun and this is done for the family when the nun is dead and in memoriam. For years I had stood and looked at these when I was walking and finally when I was writing Saint Therese in looking at these photographs I saw how Saint Therese existed from the life of an ordinary young lady to that of the nun. And so everything was actual and I went on writing. ("Plays," 130)

St. Teresa is an ideal protagonist for Stein. In a 1934 interview, Stein said she had "read the meditations of St. Therese whose mysticism was 'real and practical.'"[39] St. Teresa insisted on the participation of her body in her mystical ecstasies, and her descriptions of them are remarkable for their almost medical precision of physical detail.[40] As a religious artist of the Spanish counter-reformation, Teresa also believed in and practiced unity of body and spirit. As Robert T. Petersson says in *The Art of Ecstasy*,

With the Eucharistic Communion officially interpreted as the *actual* consuming of Christ's body and blood, many new works of art revealed body and spirit in a high degree of unity . . . The reality Teresa herself pictures in her writing is a unified state in which Creator and created exist together . . .[41]

However, it would be a mistake to equate St. Teresa's sixteenth-century religious vision with Stein's twentieth-century secular use of it. It is clear in Teresa's writing that this mystical union is a state toward which we can only aspire in this life with varying degrees of failure, while for Stein an unstrained union is the essential, constant condition of life, were we all capable of recognizing and embracing it. As Petersson says of Teresa's vision, "Man in the flesh cannot attain that unity, yet he may experience something close to it, if briefly and imperfectly."[42] In Stein's order of regained innocence, we need only be willing.

Lucy Church's dual nature is unproblematic for Stein, treated as devoid of conflict. Not so St. Teresa's predicament, her "real and practical mysticism." Teresa writes of her twenty years' battle with the ways of the world, and Stein depicts her quite appropriately as "half in and half out of doors," or "seated but not surrounded." St. Teresa's doubt is symbolic for Stein of the paradox inherent in her own vision of the simultaneity of physical and spiritual existence: of immanence — excited but earthbound movement — and the static serenity of transcendence. This conflict generates both confusion and sadness in the opera. The text continually, nervously tries to count itself: "how many acts are there in it," "how many saints are there in it," "how many saints can sit around." Like these attempts to tote up the moving parts, the comic discrepancy between the anarchic plenitude of saints and acts within the text and the pseudo-orderly enumeration of them in the title is both a gibe at orderly enumeration, and also a genuine expression of bewilderment in the face of that anarchic plenitude. This conflict also expresses itself as the familiar motif of the anxiety or sadness of mortality, of immanence, and the yearning for transcendence: "if to stay to cry," "there can be no peace on earth with calm with calm," and of course "pigeons on the grass alas." But counting stops, unity triumphs — "never to return to distinctions" — and St. Teresa's double existence finally comes to be felt not as troubling paradox but as triumphant union.

This shift is an affirmation of the female vision of Stein's "landscape" writing: the happy, easy union of the human and the physical, the spirit and the flesh, over the patriarchal mode of tragic separation and yearning. The representative of patriarchy in *Four Saints* is St. Ignatius Loyola, founder of the Jesuit sect, who is "well adapted to plans and a distance." St. Ignatius personifies detached intellect, rigorous order, and military violence. Stein thinks of him as a porcelain figure, brittle and lifeless, if charming in its ephemeral perfection:

Then in another window this time on the rue de Rennes there was a rather large porcelain group and it was of a young soldier giving alms to a beggar and taking off his helmet and his armour and leaving them in the charge of another.

It was somehow just what the young Saint Ignatius did and anyway it looked like him as I had known about him and so he too became actual not as actual as Saint Therese in the photographs but still actual and so the Four Saints got written. ("Plays," 130–131)

Stein is drawn to him, as she has been throughout her life to the qualities of what she had considered her redeeming maleness: rigor, order, detachment. But she finally prefers the gentle, pragmatically mystical, female St. Teresa.

It seems to become increasingly clear to Stein as she writes *Four Saints* that she prefers St. Teresa to St. Ignatius. As Bridgman says, "Preoccupied with Saint Theresa, Gertrude Stein made only a gesture at bringing Ignatius on stage. 'Introducing Saint Ignatius.' Then, failing to elicit any response in herself, she remarked, 'Left to be' and returned to her preferred topic: 'Saint Therese seated seated. . . .'"[43]

Actually, the first appearance of St. Ignatius, after the opening list of twenty-one saints (divided into columns according to gender—ten women and eleven men—with St. Teresa heading the women and St. Ignatius the men), is even more revealing: "Saint Ignatius not there. Saint Ignatius staying where. Never heard them speak speak of it" (*Four Saints*, 586). After "Left to be": "Saint Ignatius not standing standing surrounded . . . Did she want him dead if now" (588). Then, two pages later: "Saint Ignatius could be in porcelain actually" (590).

As this preference for St. Teresa emerges, the sense of troubled paradox in St. Teresa's situation shifts to triumphant affirmation of the unified vision: "Saint Ignatius was very well known. . . . Saint Ignatius needs not be feared. . . . Saint Ignatius finally. / Saint Ingatius well bound. / Saint Ignatius with it just. / Saint Ignatius might be read. . . . To be interested in Saint Therese fortunately" (594–595). And on the next page: "Saint Therese in place" (596).

Once St. Teresa is "in place," St. Ignatius retires into the background for the rest of the play, essentially becoming just another saint, with one final, decisive exception. He becomes important again for the pivotal "pigeons on the grass alas" sequence, as a force of separateness, dividedness, isolation. The sequence begins with his initiation of the theme "Withdrew with with withdrew. / Saint Ignatius. Occurred. / Saint Ignatius. Occurred withdrew. / Saint Ignatius. Withdrew occurred. / Saint Ignatius. Withdrew occurred. / St. Ignatius occurred St. Ignatius withdrew occurred withdrew" (603). The theme resurfaces one page later: "With withdrawn. . . . As if they liked it very well to live alone. / With withdrawn. / What can they mean by well very well" (604). The prelude to the actual "pigeons on the grass alas" aria is an interesting sequence sung by St. Ignatius, combining images of union such as "wedding" and "wide water" with strictures of time, order, isolation, defeat:

Saint Ignatius. Within it within it within it as a wedding for them in half of the time.
Saint Ignatius. Particularly.
Saint Ignatius. Call it a day.
Saint Ignatius. With a wide water with within with drawn.
Saint Ignatius. As if a fourth class. (604)

The aria itself gives us the clearest image in the libretto of the central conflict: mundane pigeons trapped on the earth, the grass, while the miraculous magpie hangs unreachable in the spiritual sky.[44] But the aria offers resolution as well: "They might be very well very well very well they might be they might be very well they might be very well very well they might be" (605), and then the soaring, untroubled invocation to purity and light: "Let Lucy Lily Lily Lucy Lucy let Lucy Lucy Lily Lily Lily Lily Lily let Lily Lucy Lucy let Lily. Let Lucy Lily" (605). Lucy and Lily are followed by a series of "Scene Ones," a complex defeat of enumeration, in which St. Ignatius's isolation is finally overcome:

SCENE ONE

Saint Ignatius and please please please please.

SCENE ONE

One and one.

SCENE ONE

Might they be with they be with them might they be with them. Never to return to distinctions. (605)

The strife and resolution are elaborated and reiterated in the next few pages, until, finally, St. Ignatius himself seems converted. In his own inimitably pompous way, he delivers a resounding affirmation of saints as an embodiment of Stein's vision of material, contingent, "circumstantial" but at the same time "fundamental," or eternal, oneness:

Saint Ignatius. Foundationally marvellously aboundingly illimitably with it as a circumstance. Fundamentally and saints fundamentally and saints and fundamentally and saints. (607)

The prolific and successful operas and plays of the thirties and forties, most of them in *Last Operas and Plays* (*Listen to Me, A Play Called Not and Now, Doctor Faustus Lights the Lights, Yes Is for a Very Young Man, The Mother of Us All*), clearly derive in structure from *Four Saints*, and most of them could be put to music just as successfully (some of them have been).[45] Stein's only other operatic collaboration with Thomson was *The Mother of Us All*, another celebration of the female, this time embodied — differently but at least as appropriately — in Susan B. Anthony. This heroine dies having failed in her goal of female suffrage, and returns as a statue, singing, in a way that must be, for Stein, autobiographical, of Anthony's "long life of strife." *The Mother of Us All* was, fittingly, Stein's last work. One can only agree with Virgil Thomson:

Putting to music poetry so musically conceived as Gertrude Stein's has long been a pleasure to me. The spontaneity of it, its easy flow, and its deep sincerity have always seemed to me just right for music. Whether my music is just right for it is not for me to say. But happiness was ours working together, and a great friendship grew up between us. This friendship lasted twenty years, till her death.

Her last completed work was another libretto written for me, *The Mother of Us All*. That too became an opera and was produced, but Gertrude Stein never saw it. I am sorry now that I did not write an opera with her every year. It had not occurred to me that both of us would not always be living.[46]

Conclusion

G ertrude Stein's career has the sort of tidy contour that invites (seduces) tidy summation. A psychobiographical summation would have her withdrawing, after *Three Lives*, from clear expression of her guilty sexual feeling into the safety and privacy of hermetic experimentalism, but emerging from it in the thirties, purged of neurosis by fame, ready to communicate again. This analysis accounts for the facts, but not for its own bias in favor of conventional writing; also, it entirely omits the historical, political, intellectual components and implications of the pattern it identifies.

Catharine Stimpson gives us an important historical-political component: the extremely difficult situation, in the early twentieth century, of intellectual women, and particularly lesbians, in a society which considered them at best barely capable of the intellectual life and at worst a "pollutant." This historical-political context enables us to see Stein's experimental writing as a location of her literary rebellion, against the patriarchal structures which excluded her, in language itself rather than in thematic content. Expressed as content, this rebellion would have been both too threateningly explicit and also, paradoxically, less extreme. If patriarchy is to be transformed at all, it must be transformed not only at its most visible levels (political, social, economic, cultural) but also at the fundamental or radical level of the structures of language which enable meaning.

Stein's linguistic or literary rebellion is not solitary. As Kristeva allows us to see, it is part of the general twentieth-century rebellion of the avant-garde against patriarchal structures of art and thought, a rebellion which places the avant-garde, and particularly experimental writing, in the location of women: patriarchy's repressed Other, and therefore its antidote. The shape of Stein's experimental career is in fact quite neatly in tune with the history of the avant-garde in this century: blossoming (erupting) in the prewar years, fading during World War I, coming into its own in the twenties, retreating (though never entirely) in the face of the overriding political, social, and economic crises of the thirties and forties. Had her life been as long as the century's, one can imagine her emerging as a leader of the avant-garde's resurgence in the late fifties, the sixties, and the seventies, when "postmodernists" began to do what she, almost alone, had done fifty years before.

But she did die in 1946, and there has been a tendency to see her later work as a recovery of her senses. The neat model of Stein's career as a trajectory from the conventional early prose of *Fernhurst* and *Q.E.D.* through increasingly radical degrees of experimentalism, reaching an apogee sometime in the teens and early twenties, and then gradually returning to the conventional fold, is an over-simplification, a distortion. Most of her work in the thirties and forties is, or is almost, conventionally readable, but it does not represent a repudiation of or release from experimental writing. As rapprochement of the experimental with the conventional, it represents, instead, precisely Kristeva's ideal alternation of the male and the female psychological-linguistic-political modes — her sense that we need a "paternal identification" (time, reason, history), that we must not isolate ourselves within a female identity once we have retrieved it. If we see Stein's work between 1906 and 1932 as, literally, the creation of a plausible, largely successful body of anti-patriarchal literature, we can see her work in the thirties and forties as producing, both within itself and in relation to her earlier work, Kristeva's "impossible dialectic," the "constant alternation between time and its 'truth,' identity and its loss, history and the timeless, signless, extra-phenomenal things that produce it" (one thinks immediately of *Mrs. Reynolds, Ida, Wars I Have Seen, The Mother of Us All*). In her radical experimental writing, Stein creates a polymorphous language which points to a culture beyond "phallogocentrism," beyond patriarchy; her work of the thirties and forties shows us that such a utopian language and culture can, as Barthes says in a different formulation of what is essentially the same dialectic, situate itself "in *this world*":

Is our literature forever doomed to this exhausting oscillation between political realism and art-for-art's-sake, between an ethic of commitment and an esthetic purism, between compromise and asepsis? Must it always be poor (if it is merely itself) or embarrassed (if it is anything but itself)? Can it not have a proper place in *this world*?"[1]

NOTES

INDEX

Notes

Introduction

1 By the use of the word "interpretation" I do not mean to invoke the current debate over the proper sphere of critical activity: whether criticism should be engaged in elucidating (interpreting) particular texts, or whether it should focus on developing a comprehensive theory of literary discourse, a "poetics" of literature. Jonathan Culler advocates the latter position in his essay "Beyond Interpretation," *Comparative Literature* 28 (1976), 244–256; and the Society for Critical Exchange's *SCE Reports* 6 (Fall 1979) gives several critics' responses to Culler's argument. I use "interpretation" here to mean the formulation of thematic synthesis or configurative meaning as the primary response to a literary text. Susan Sontag uses the word in the same way in the famous essay to which my argument is indebted: "Against Interpretation," in *Against Interpretation* (New York: Farrar, Straus & Giroux, 1966), 13–23.

2 A selected list of such criticism: Mabel Dodge, "Speculation, or Post-Impressionism in Prose," *Arts and Decoration* 3 (1913), 172–174; L. T. Fitz, "Gertrude Stein and Picasso: The Language of Surfaces," *Ameri-*

can *Literature* 45 (May 1973), 228–237; Samuel H. McMillan, "Gertrude Stein, the Cubists, and the Futurists," Ph.D. diss., University of Texas, 1964; Marilyn Gaddis Rose, "Gertrude Stein and the Cubist Narrative," *Modern Fiction Studies* 22 (1976–77), 543–555; Wendy Steiner, *Exact Resemblance to Exact Resemblance: The Literary Portraiture of Gertrude Stein* (New Haven: Yale University Press, 1978); Wylie Sypher, *Rococo to Cubism in Art and Literature* (New York: Random House, 1963); William Wasserstrom, "The Sursymamericubealism of Gertrude Stein," *Twentieth Century Literature* 21 (February 1975), 90–106. The most recent treatment of Stein's work from this point of view, and an extremely sophisticated, persuasive argument, is Marjorie Perloff, "Poetry as Word-System: The Art of Gertrude Stein," *American Poetry Review* 8:5 (Sept./Oct. 1979), 33–43.

3 In her groundbreaking article "The Mind, the Body and Gertrude Stein," *Critical Inquiry* 3:3 (Spring 1977), 489–506, Catharine Stimpson analyzes in Stein's literary work her strategy for coping with the culturally imposed split between her intellect and her sexuality. Elizabeth Fifer proceeds from Stimpson's work in "Is Flesh Advisable? The Interior Theater of Gertrude Stein," *Signs* 4:3 (Spring 1979), 472–483.

4 The most important essays are the six *Lectures in America* (New York: Random House, 1935), hereafter cited as *Lectures in America*; "Composition as Explanation" of 1926 in *Selected Writings of Gertrude Stein*, ed. Carl Van Vechten (New York: Random House, 1946), hereafter cited as *Selected Writings*; "How Writing is Written" of 1935, in *How Writing is Written*, ed. Robert Bartlett Haas (Los Angeles: Black Sparrow Press, 1974); *What Are Master-pieces* (1935; rpt. Los Angeles: Conference Press, 1940) (The edition that I used and cite elsewhere in this book is: "What Are Master-pieces," *Gertrude Stein: Writings and Lectures 1909–1945*, ed. Patricia Meyerowitz [Harmondsworth, Eng.: Penguin, 1967].); *Narration* (Chicago: University of Chicago Press, 1935); and *Picasso* (New York: Scribners, 1940).

5 Donald Sutherland, *Gertrude Stein: A Biography of Her Work* (New Haven: Yale University Press, 1951), hereafter cited as Sutherland, *Gertrude Stein*.

6 Richard Bridgman, *Gertrude Stein in Pieces* (New York: Oxford University Press, 1970), hereafter cited as Bridgman, *Gertrude Stein in Pieces*.

7 See Allegra Stewart, *Gertrude Stein and the Present* (Cambridge, Mass.: Harvard University Press, 1967) for the most inclusive discussion of Stein's connections to early modern philosophy.

8 Norman Weinstein, *Gertrude Stein and the Literature of Modern Consciousness* (New York: Ungar, 1970).

9 This undervaluation is a tendency, not all-encompassing, in Bridgman's book. He also interests himself in the nature and effect of Stein's linguistic innovations for their own sake, apart from their psychosexual origins, particularly in his discussion of *Tender Buttons*.

10 Stimpson, "The Mind, the Body and Gertrude Stein," 498–499.

11 Fifer, "Is Flesh Advisable?" 482.

12 Steiner, *Exact Resemblance to Exact Resemblance*, 94.

13 Ibid., 101.

14 The work of Neil Schmitz, William Gass, and Marjorie Perloff have been particularly sensitive to Stein's radical re-creation of language. Professor Perloff's work on Stein (see also her chapter on Stein in *The Poetics of Indeterminacy* [Princeton: Princeton University Press, 1981]), identifies it as indeterminate or polysemous, though her focus is on using the idea of indeterminacy to show how many readings we can generate from a particular work (she analyzes "Susie Asado" in detail) rather than on the cultural or political implications of indeterminacy. Neil Schmitz does treat the anti-patriarchal implications of Stein's work in "Portrait, Patriarchy, Mythos: The Revenge of Gertrude Stein" (*Salmagundi* [Summer 1978], 70–91), in which he shows how Stein's version of herself in *The Autobiography of Alice B. Toklas* eludes and remakes partriarchal stereotypes of women.

Chapter 1: Experimental Writing

1 Donald Barthelme, "Bone Bubbles," *City Life* (New York: Bantam, 1971), 125.

2 James Joyce, *Finnegans Wake* (New York: Viking, 1939), 468.

3 William Burroughs, *Nova Express* (New York: Grove, 1964), 72.

4 Virginia Woolf, "Monday or Tuesday," *A Haunted House and Other Short Stories* (New York: Harcourt, Brace & World, 1949), 6–7.

5 Samuel Beckett, "Ping," *First Love and Other Shorts* (New York: Grove, 1974), 71.

6 Gertrude Stein, "In Between," *Tender Buttons*, in *Selected Writings*, 472–473.

7 J. Hillis Miller, "Deconstructing the Deconstructors," *Diacritics* 5:2 (Summer 1975), 24–31; quote is from 31.

8 Some references: Monroe Beardsley, *The Possibility of Criticism* (Detroit: Wayne State University Press, 1970); E. D. Hirsch, *The Aims of Interpretation* (Chicago: University of Chicago Press, 1975);

George L. Dillon, *Language Processing and the Reading of Literature* (Bloomington: Indiana University Press, 1978); Tzvetan Todorov, *The Poetics of Prose* (Ithaca: Cornell University Press, 1977); Norman Holland, *The Dynamics of the Literary Response* (New York: Norton, 1975); Geoffrey Hartman, "The Interpreter: A Self-Analysis," in *The Fate of Reading* (Chicago: University of Chicago Press, 1975), 3–19; Paul Ricoeur, *The Rule of Metaphor* (Toronto: University of Toronto Press, 1978) and "The Metaphorical Process," *Critical Inquiry* 5:1 (Autumn 1978), 143–59; and of course Erich Auerbach, *Mimesis* (Princeton: Princeton University Press, 1953).

9 Jonathan Culler, *Structuralist Poetics* (Ithaca: Cornell University Press, 1975).

10 Again, I do not use "interpretation" here as Culler uses it in his later essay, "Beyond Interpretation" (see Introduction, n.1).

11 Culler, *Structuralist Poetics*, 114.

12 Ibid., 113.

13 George Steiner, "'Critic'/'Reader'," *New Literary History* 10:3 (Spring 1979), 423.

14 Harold Bloom, *The Visionary Company* (New York: Doubleday, 1961), 42; quoted in Culler, *Structuralist Poetics*, 115.

15 Wolfgang Iser, "The Reading Process: A Phenomenological Approach," in *The Implied Reader: Patterns of Communication in Prose Fiction from Bunyan to Beckett* (Baltimore: Johns Hopkins University Press, 1974), 283. This essay is at the center of Iser's thought: it contains the most succinct formulation of his ideas.

16 Wolfgang Iser, *The Act of Reading* (Baltimore: Johns Hopkins University Press, 1979).

17 Noam Chomsky, "Some Methodological Remarks on Generative Grammar," *Word* 17 (1961), 219–239.

18 Ibid., 221.

19 Ibid., 222.

20 Gertrude Stein, "Portraits and Repetition," *Lectures in America*, 202.

21 Gertrude Stein, "Pictures," *Lectures in America*, 84.

22 Gertrude Stein, "What Are Master-pieces," *Gertrude Stein: Writings and Lectures 1909–1945*, 150.

23 Gertrude Stein, "Portrait of Mabel Dodge at the Villa Curonia," *Selected Writings*, 528. This sentence is characteristic of Stein's "lively words" writing, 1911–13, one of her most important and successful experimental styles.

24 I am not quoting any particular critic, but I do not think these sentences significantly exaggerate the spirit of the translating approach.

25 Roland Barthes, *The Pleasure of the Text*, trans. Richard Miller (New York: Farrar, Straus & Giroux, 1975).

26 Ibid., 42.

27 Notebook numbered by Stein "MA," p. 47, Notebooks of Gertrude Stein in Yale Collection of American Literature, Beinecke Rare Book and Manuscript Library, Yale University Library.

28 Jacques Derrida, *Of Grammatology*, trans. Gayatri Chakravorty Spivak (Baltimore: Johns Hopkins University Press, 1974).

29 Roland Barthes, "From Work to Text," *Textual Strategies*, ed. Josué V. Harari (Ithaca: Cornell University Press, 1979), 76–77 (originally published in *Revue d'Esthétique* 3 [1971] as "de l'oeuvre au texte").

30 Derrida, *Of Grammatology*, 87.

31 Ibid., 86.

32 Ibid., 85.

33 This word appears in Derrida's "The Purveyor of the Truth," trans. W. Domingo, J. Hulbert, M. Ron, and M.-R. Logan, *Yale French Studies* 52 (1975), 96: "Freud, like those who follow him here, does nothing else but describe the necessity of phallogocentrism, explain its effects, which are as obvious as they are massive. Phallogocentrism is neither an accident nor a speculative mistake which may be imputed to this or that theoretician. It is an enormous old root ('so to speak') which must also be accounted for." See also Derrida, *Spurs: Nietzsche's Styles*, trans. Barbara Harlow (Chicago: University of Chicago Press, 1979).

34 See Hélène Cixous, "Sorties," *La Jeune Née* (Paris: Union Générale d'Éditions, 10/18, 1975), and "Le rire de la méduse," *L'arc* (1975) 39–54; Luce Irigaray, *Speculum de l'autre femme* (Paris: Éditions de Minuit, 1974) and *Ce sexe qui n'en est pas un* (Paris: Éditions de Minuit, 1977). Extracts from these and many other works of current French feminist theory are published in translation in *New French Feminisms*, ed. Elaine Marks and Isabelle de Courtivron (Amherst: University of Massachusetts Press, 1980). See also Elaine Marks, "Review: French Literary Criticism," and Carolyn Greenstein Burke, "Report from Paris: Women's Writing and the Women's Movement," *Signs* 3:4 (Summer 1978), 832–855; *Women Writing and Writing about Women*, ed. Mary Jacobus (London: Croom Helm, 1979); *The Future of Difference*, ed. Hester Eisenstein and Alice Jardine (Boston: G. K. Hall, 1980); Ann Rosalind Jones, "Writing the Body: Toward An Understanding of L'Écriture Féminine," Hélène Vivienne Wenzel, "The Text as Body/Politics: An Appreciation of Monique Wittig's Writings in Context," and Carolyn Burke, "Irigaray Through the

Looking Glass," *Feminist Studies* 7:2 (Summer 1981), 247–306; *Yale French Studies* 62 (1981) entitled: "Feminist Readings: French Texts/American Contexts"; *Signs* 7:1 (Autumn 1981) entitled: "French Feminist Theory"; *Critical Inquiry* 8:2 (Winter 1981) entitled: "Writing and Sexual Difference."

35 See also D. W. Winnicott, *Playing and Reality* (New York: Basic Books, 1971).

36 See particularly "The Agency of the letter in the unconscious or reason since Freud," and "The signification of the phallus," in *Écrits: A Selection*, trans. Alan Sheridan (New York: Norton, 1977), 146–178, 281–291.

37 Gertrude Stein, "Preciosilla," in *Selected Writings*, 550–551.

38 Julia Kristeva, "Oscillation du 'pouvoir' au 'refus,'" interview by Xavière Gauthier in *Tel Quel* (Summer 1974), trans. Marilyn A. August as "Oscillation between Power and Denial," *New French Feminisms*, 165.

39 Julia Kristeva, *About Chinese Women*, trans. Anita Barrows (London: Marion Boyars, 1977), 29–30. For a hard look at Kristeva's evidence and argument in *About Chinese Women* and in her *Tel Quel* writing, see Gayatri Chakravorty Spivak, "French Feminism in an International Frame," *Yale French Studies* 62 (1981), 154–184, especially 157–164. While I agree with Spivak's critique of Kristeva's anthropological evidence, and of the overall rigor of her demonstrations, I do not agree that we should therefore dismiss Kristeva's conclusions. Those conclusions are based on ideas which one can reject, as one can reject Marx or Freud, but which are nonetheless powerful theoretical models of culture, and do not depend for their legitimacy on the rigor of any one writer's presentation of them. For more of Kristeva's psychology of language, see *Desire in Language* (New York: Columbia University Press, 1980), and *Polylogue* (Paris: Seuil, 1977).

40 Kristeva, *About Chinese Women*, 40.

41 Kristeva, ibid., 38.

42 Ibid.

43 Ibid., 14.

44 Ibid., 37–38.

45 Again, experimental writing represents an actual "maternal identification" only to the extent that it employs presymbolic modes of signification. Otherwise, experimental writing is "maternal" only in that it opposes the language of patriarchy.

46 I qualify this assertion ("*most* experimental texts") because some purely aural modes of Stein's are quite successful.

47 The most important of these are "Composition as Explanation," *Lectures in America*, *The Geographical History of America*, *Narration*, "How Writing Is Written," "What Are Master-pieces," and *Picasso*.
48 Gertrude Stein, "What is English Literature," *Lectures in America*, 16.

Chapter 2: *Three Lives*

1 Weinstein, *Gertrude Stein and the Literature of Modern Consciousness*.
2 Bridgman, *Gertrude Stein in Pieces*, 57.
3 Michael Hoffman, *Gertrude Stein*, Twayne's United States Authors Series, ed. Sylvia E. Bowman (Boston: Twayne, 1976), 21.
4 Conrad's Marlow, Ford's Dowell, Faulkner's Quentin, Fitzgerald's Nick Carraway, etc.
5 Gertrude Stein, *Three Lives* (1909; rpt. New York: Random House, 1936), 242-243.
6 Gertrude Stein, *Q.E.D.*, in *Fernhurst, Q.E.D., and Other Early Writings* (New York: Liveright, 1971). The similarity between *Q.E.D.* and *Melanctha* has been demonstrated and discussed by Bridgman in *Gertrude Stein in Pieces* (52-54); Leon Katz, in his introduction to *Fernhurst, Q.E.D., and Other Early Writings* (ix-xx); and Catharine Stimpson in "The Mind, the Body and Gertrude Stein," 499-502.
7 For a full account of this affair and of its fictionalization in *Q.E.D.*, see Katz's introduction to *Fernhurst, Q.E.D., and Other Early Writings*.
8 See particularly Elaine Showalter, *A Literature of Their Own* (Princeton: Princeton University Press, 1977), and Sandra M. Gilbert and Susan Gubar, *The Madwoman in the Attic* (New Haven: Yale University Press, 1979).
9 This term was invented by Joseph Frank in his famous essay "Spatial Form in Modern Literature," *Sewanee Review* (1945). See also Sharon Spencer, *Space, Time and Structure in the Modern Novel* (Chicago: Swallow Press, 1971), and Patricia Tobin, *Time and the Novel: The Genealogical Imperative* (Princeton: Princeton University Press, 1978).
10 Stimpson, "The Mind, the Body and Gertrude Stein," 493.
11 Stein mentions her rebellion, using the word "revolt," several times (p. 29 of the notebook numbered "2" by Professor Katz) in the notebooks; i.e., "Leon like me in ideas and revolt." (Leon is Leon Solomons, her close friend and coworker in William James's laboratory at Harvard, on whom the character of David Hersland in *The Making of Americans* is partly based.)

12 This remark appears in a late notebook: p. 21 of the notebook labeled "C" by Stein.

13 Richard Poirier, *A World Elsewhere* (New York: Oxford University Press, 1966), 5.

14 See Tobin, *Time and the Novel.*

15 Sutherland, *Gertrude Stein,* 38.

16 Bruce Kawin, *Telling It Again and Again* (Ithaca: Cornell University Press, 1972).

17 See for example Edward D. Snyder, *Hypnotic Poetry* (1930; rpt. New York: Octagon Books, 1971).

Chapter 3: Insistence

1 These periods, as listed in his Appendix, are "Naturalism and the Continuous Present, 1902–1911," "The Visible World as Simply Different, 1911–*ca.* 1921," "The Visible World with Movement (First Plays), 1913–1922," "The Play as Movement and Landscape, 1922–1932," "The Melodic Drama, Melodrama, and Opera, 1922–1946," "Calligraphy and Melody, 1920–1932," "Syntax as Movement, Vibration and Drawing, 1928–1940," and "History and Legend, 1920–1946." Sutherland, *Gertrude Stein,* 205–209.

2 Bridgman mentions the first three styles (which I call "insistence," "lively words," and "voices"), and emphasizes the importance of studying Stein's chronological development, but organizes his text by work rather than style. His focus on individual works obscures the larger groupings.

3 Bridgman's invaluable Appendix C, "Key to the *Yale Catalogue,* Part 4," *Gertrude Stein in Pieces,* 365–385, makes the dates of authorship readily available.

4 Until 1908 she had been working on it exclusively; between 1908 and 1911 she worked on several other projects as well (Bridgman, *Gertrude Stein in Pieces,* 91).

5 Transcripts of these unpublished notebooks, the originals of which are currently being edited for publication by Professor Leon Katz, are in the Yale Collection of American Literature at the Beinecke Rare Book and Manuscript Library of Yale University.

6 This remark appears early in the notebooks, on p. 27 of the notebook numbered "6" by Professor Katz.

7 Gertrude Stein, *The Making of Americans* (New York: Harcourt, Brace, 1934), 215. This is the abridged edition, but abridged by Stein herself in 1934 along the lines of Bernard Faÿ's French translation. I

use it because it is readily available in paperback; also, though this abridgment is not ideal, I do not think it sacrifices much.

8 Gertrude Stein, *Two: Gertrude Stein and Her Brother, and Other Early Portraits* (New Haven: Yale University Press, 1951), 349–350.

9 Roland Barthes, *S/Z*, trans. Richard Miller (New York: Farrar, Straus & Giroux, 1974), 4.

10 David Lodge, in *The Modes of Modern Writing: Metaphor, Metonymy, and the Typology of Modern Literature* (Ithaca: Cornell University Press, 1977), 144–154, uses Roman Jakobson's division of literature into the metaphoric and metonymic axes to discuss Stein's early experimental work as alternately carrying each axis as far as it can go while at the same time entirely subverting or ignoring the other. What I call "insistence" is seen by Lodge as an extreme of the metonymic axis, while the "lively words" style of *Tender Buttons* is an extreme of the metaphoric axis. The extensive use of pronouns and what Lodge calls "all-purpose substitute words" (148) are evidence, according to Jakobson's theory, of the dominance of the metonymic axis. According to Lodge, modern literature is generally metonymic.

11 Gertrude Stein, *Matisse, Picasso and Gertrude Stein* (also known as *G.M.P.*) (1933; rpt. Millerton, N.Y.: Something Else Press, 1972), 207.

12 See for example "Julia Marlowe" or "Harriet Fear" in *Two*, or "Storyette H.M." in *Portraits and Prayers* (New York: Random House, 1934).

13 There are many of these, such as "A Man," "Five or Six Men," "Purrmann" in *Two*; the famous "Matisse" and "Picasso" in *Portraits and Prayers*; "Ada," "Miss Furr and Miss Skeene," "Italians" in *Geography and Plays* (1922; rpt. New York: Something Else Press, 1968), hereafter cited as *Geography and Plays*. (The above is a partial list.)

14 All in *Two*. Some others: the first parts of "Jenny, Helen, Hannah, Paul and Peter" and of "Orta or One Dancing" in *Two*, or "Mi-Careme" in *Portraits and Prayers*. This problem pervades the long narratives.

15 This is the core of "A Kind of Women," *Two*, 321. See also "Elise Surville" and "Hessel" in *Two*. Again, this problem is worst and most pervasive in the long narratives, particularly *Many Many Women*.

16 Other successful portraits, both in this period, such as "Frost" in *Two*, and later, such as the famous "Susie Asado" in *Geography and Plays*, employ a circular structure.

17 This remark is in a late notebook, on p. 11 of the notebook labeled "D" by Stein.

Chapter 4: Lively Words

1 Gertrude Stein, *Many Many Women*, in *Matisse, Picasso and Gertrude Stein with Two Shorter Stories* (1933; rpt. Millerton, N.Y.: Something Else Press, 1972), 175.

2 She was definitely writing in the new style by the time she visited Mabel Dodge in Florence in the summer of 1911.

3 Gertrude Stein, "Portrait of Constance Fletcher," *Geography and Plays*, 159.

4 Neil Schmitz, "Gertrude Stein as Post-Modernist: The Rhetoric of *Tender Buttons*," *Journal of Modern Literature* 3:5 (July 1974), 1203-1218.

5 Leo Stein, *Journal into the Self: Being the Letters, Papers and Journals of Leo Stein*, ed. Edmund Fuller (New York: Crown, 1950), 48.

6 Mabel Dodge was so taken with the portrait that she had three hundred copies bound and distributed among friends in 1912 and wrote a favorable article about Stein for the 1913 New York Armory Show. That show brought cubism to America, and was the beginning of Stein's reputation. Bridgman sees "no intrinsic reason for the celebrity of Mabel Dodge's portrait" (121), but I think it is a successful example of the early "lively words" style.

7 Ibid., 49.

8 André Breton and Philippe Soupault discovered that fact in their experiment in automatic writing, *Les Champs Magnétiques* (Paris: Au Sans-Pareil, 1921).

9 In one place she says she wrote "Food" and "Rooms" when she returned to Paris; in another she says she "described rooms and objects" (Bridgman, 125). This tells me that, by 1932, she simply could not remember what she wrote when. If the order of composition were the same as the order of publication, she would not have had that trouble. Also, Stein composed *Tender Buttons* in three separate notebooks, the first labeled "Food," the second "Rooms," and the third "Objects." Each appears to be written consecutively; none of them is filled. It seems logical to assume that she worked on them simultaneously. (The Stein manuscripts are in the Yale Collection of American Literature at Beinecke Rare Book and Manuscript Library, Yale University Library, New Haven, Conn.)

10 Gertrude Stein, *Tender Buttons, Selected Writings*, 499.

11 Sutherland, *Gertrude Stein*, 84. Bridgman says "Even a loyalist like Donald Sutherland was reduced to describing it as a 'sort of Wonderland or Luna Park for anyone who is not too busy.'" *Gertrude Stein in Pieces*, 125.

12 Stein says of portrait writing "I must find out what is moving inside them that makes them them, and I must find out how I by the thing moving excitedly inside in me can make a portrait of them." ("Portraits and Repetition," *Lectures in America*, 183.

13 The experimental playwright-director Richard Foreman, who acknowledges his debt to Stein, describes a very similar process of composition. See Kate Davy, "Richard Foreman's Ontological-Hysterical Theatre: The Influence of Gertrude Stein," *Twentieth Century Literature* 24:1 (Spring 1978), 118.

14 Some other successful late "lively words" portraits: "A Sweet Tail (Gypsies)," "One (Van Vechten)," in *Geography and Plays*; "Guillaume Apollinaire," "Mrs. Edwardes," in *Portraits and Prayers*; "Preciosilla," in *Selected Writings*.

15 Gertrude Stein, "Susie Asado," *Geography and Plays*, 13. See Marjorie Perloff, "Poetry as Word-System: The Art of Gertrude Stein," *American Poetry Review* 8:5 (Sept./Oct. 1979), 33–43, for a close reading of irreducibly multiple meaning in "Susie Asado."

Chapter 5: Voices and Plays

1 Gertrude Stein, "Plays," *Lectures in America*, 119.

2 Gertrude Stein, "What Happened," *Geography and Plays*, 205.

3 Gertrude Stein, "White Wines," *Geography and Plays*, 210.

4 Gertrude Stein, "A Curtain Raiser," *Geography and Plays*, 202.

5 Gertrude Stein, "The Gradual Making of the Making of Americans," *Lectures in America*, 98.

6 Drama is commonly believed to originate in primitive religious ceremonies. Luminaries of avant-garde theatre such as Antonin Artaud and Jerzy Grotowski construct their theories on that premise.

7 "More in" is also a favorite phrase of this period. Each Steinian period has its own repertoire of favorite words and phrases, an extension of the "words with really existing being." Bridgman follows them through Stein's career.

8 Gertrude Stein, "Sacred Emily," *Geography and Plays*, 178.

9 Gertrude Stein, "I Have No Title to Be Successful," *Painted Lace and Other Pieces (1914–1937)* (New Haven: Yale University Press, 1955), 23, hereafter cited as *Painted Lace.*

10 A case might be made for viewing these private narratives of daily trivia as a valorization or even celebration of female experience. The danger of such an argument, in my opinion, is not only that it makes a virtue of necessity, but that it insists unnecessarily on valorizing *all* female experience, no matter what its nature. Surely we do not

want to argue that all female experience, in patriarchy, is worth celebrating.

11 Barthes, *The Pleasure of the Text*, 49.

12 Gertrude Stein, "He Didn't Light the Light," *Painted Lace*, 17.

13 Gertrude Stein, "Do Let Us Go Away. A Play," *Geography and Plays*, 215.

14 Gertrude Stein, "Mexico," *Geography and Plays*, 310.

15 Gertrude Stein, "An Exercise in Analysis," *Last Operas and Plays* (1949; rpt. New York: Random House, 1975), 119.

16 Gertrude Stein, "Exceptional Conduct," *Bee Time Vine and Other Pieces (1913–1927)* (New Haven: Yale University Press, 1953), 207–208, hereafter cited as *Bee Time Vine*.

Chapter 6: Melody

1 Gertrude Stein, *The Autobiography of Alice B. Toklas* (New York: Random House, 1933), 206.

2 Gertrude Stein, "Polish," *Bee Time Vine*, 215.

3 "POLISH (also 1919) is about Poland and current events. V.T." *Bee Time Vine*, 215.

4 Gertrude Stein, "Mary," *Bee Time Vine*, 223.

5 Gertrude Stein, "A Hymn," *Bee Time Vine*, 215.

6 In *On the Margins of Discourse* (Chicago: University of Chicago Press, 1978), Barbara Herrnstein Smith argues

that from our earliest years, indeed from the very beginnings of our lives as verbal creatures, we find sources of fascination and pleasure in language that are largely (though probably not altogether) independent of its instrumental functions. Infants apparently find inherently gratifying their own imitation of the linguistic sounds they hear, and young children seem universally to take delight not only in storytelling, songs, and verbal impersonation, but also in producing and hearing rhythmic or repeated linguistic sounds and, later, in puns, riddles, paradoxes, and other kinds of formal and thematic wordplay. One may speculate on the developmental origins and functions of such wordplay, noting, for example, that it allows children to rehearse and exercise those skills required for the use of language in the marketplace: perceptual and cognitive, as well as motor, skills. It seems clear, however, that our interest and pleasure in exploring the properties of language, and also in exploring our own responses to it, do not disappear when we come of age, and that we continue throughout our lives to make excursions from the marketplaces to the playgrounds of language. (125)

7 Gertrude Stein, "Sonnets That Please", *Bee Time Vine*, 220.

8 Gertrude Stein, "Plays," *Lectures in America*, 119. See Chapter 5, n. 1.

9 Some of it in America: the fiction of E. L. Doctorow, Kurt Vonnegut, Robert Coover, Richard Brautigan (other readers might certainly have different lists and/or object to mine).

10 Norman Holland, *Dynamics of the Literary Response* (New York: Norton, 1975).

11 Gertrude Stein, "Before the Flowers of Friendship Faded Friendship Faded," in *Gertrude Stein: Writings and Lectures 1909–1945*, 274.

12 Gertrude Stein, "Stanzas in Meditation," *Stanzas in Meditation and Other Poems (1929–1933)* (New Haven: Yale University Press, 1956), 8–9.

13 Gertrude Stein, "A Valentine to Sherwood Anderson," *Writings and Lectures*, 225.

14 Andrew Welsh, *Roots of Lyric* (Princeton: Princeton University Press, 1978).

15 Welsh, *Roots of Lyric*, 154–155.

16 Ibid., 195.

17 Ibid., 153.

18 Gertrude Stein, "The Fifteenth of November. A Portrait of T. S. Eliot," *Portraits and Prayers* (New York: Random House, 1934), 72.

19 Gertrude Stein, "If I Told Him. A Completed Portrait of Picasso," *Gertrude Stein: Writings and Lectures 1909 – 1945*, 230.

Chapter 7: Landscape

1 Gertrude Stein, "A Description of the Fifteenth of November. A Portrait of T. S. Eliot," *Portraits and Prayers*, 68.

2 Gertrude Stein, "Talks to Saints or Stories of Saint Remy," *Painted Lace*, 112.

3 George Orwell, "Politics and the English Language," *Inside the Whale and Other Essays* (1956; rpt, 1962, Harmondsworth: Penguin, 1960), 143–158.

4 Gertrude Stein, *A Novel of Thank You* (New Haven: Yale University Press, 1958), 122.

5 "I said then that sentences as they have for centuries been written were a balancing a complete inner balance of something that stated something as being existing and that a paragraph was a succession of these sentences that going on and then stopping made the emotional

content of something having a beginning and middle and ending."
Gertrude Stein, *Narration*, 20.

6 Gertrude Stein, *How to Write* (1931; rpt. West Glover, Vt.: Something Else Press, 1973).

7 Gertrude Stein, "Felicity in Moonlight. A Traveler's Story," 1927, *Painted Lace*, 65.

8 Gertrude Stein, "Separated," 1921, *Bee Time Vine*, 221.

9 Gertrude Stein, "Not A Hole," 1921, *Bee Time Vine*, 223.

10 Gertrude Stein, "Arthur A Grammar," *How to Write*, 39.

11 Gertrude Stein, "Natural Phenomena," *Painted Lace*, 220.

12 Gertrude Stein, "How Writing is Written," *How Writing is Written: Volume II of the Previously Uncollected Writings of Gertrude Stein*, ed. Robert Bartlett Haas (Los Angeles: Black Sparrow Press, 1974), 152–153.

13 Stein, "Plays," 125. This passage makes clear Stein's intellectual indebtedness to her intimate, detailed knowledge of painting.

14 Gertrude Stein, "Patriarchal Poetry," *Bee Time Vine*, 249–294.

15 See Sandra M. Gilbert and Susan Gubar, *The Madwoman in the Attic* (New Haven: Yale University Press, 1979).

16 I hesitate to claim categorically that all of "Patriarchical Poetry" defies interpretation because, by using the title as a passkey, one might contrive to interpret some passages. However, as Stanley Fish has shown ("How to Recognize a Poem When You See One," talk given at Columbia University Conference "Languages of Knowledge and of Inquiry," April 17–18, 1980), if one is given a meaning in advance, or even the assumption that meaning must be present, one can then read that meaning into almost anything (Fish's students were able to interpret thematically, in numerous ways, a simple list of surnames, described to them as a "poem").

17 There is no evidence that Stein considered conventional writing patriarchal. She might simply have found the phrase both amusingly pretentious and suggestively abstract.

18 Sutherland, *Gertrude Stein*, 131.

19 Ibid., 143.

20 Bridgman, *Gertrude Stein in Pieces*, 176.

21 Ibid., 84.

22 Ibid., 190.

23 Ibid., 192n.

24 Gertrude Stein, *Lucy Church Amiably* (1930; rpt. N.Y.: Something Else Press, 1969), 47.

25 Sutherland, *Gertrude Stein*, 121.

26 Ibid., 139.
27 Bridgman, *Gertrude Stein in Pieces*, 190.
28 Sutherland, *Gertrude Stein*, 122–123.
29 Adrienne Rich, Susan Griffin, Mary Daly; Luce Irigaray, Hélène Cixous, Monique Wittig.
30 Gertrude Stein, *Fernhurst*, in *Fernhurst, Q.E.D. and Other Early Writings* (New York: Liveright, 1971), 3–8.
31 This remark appears in a late notebook: p. 21 of the notebook labeled "C" by Stein. Stein had been discussing Toklas for quite a while, and her opinion of her had shifted from "Alice runs herself by her intellect but there is not enough intellect in her to go around and so she fails in every way" (DB–56–3), to "the slender white stem soul" (Ⓑ–13) and "sensitive, crooked, good at bottom" (Ⓑ–15). This shift in feeling toward Alice coincides with a clear shift in Stein's gender identity, from "my actual sexual nature is pure servant female" (Ⓒ–30) to the "Moi aussi, perhaps" cited above.
32 As Catharine Stimpson says in "The Mind, the Body and Gertrude Stein," "Consistently, Stein's language of self was male and masculine" (496).
33 Gertrude Stein, *Mrs. Reynolds* (New Haven: Yale University Press, 1952), 140.
34 Gertrude Stein, *Four Saints in Three Acts*, in Selected Writings of Gertrude Stein, 586.
35 "The reputation of the piece is maintained by external considerations: Virgil Thomson's musical score; the publicity surrounding the original staging of the opera in 1934 and its revival in 1952; the use of a black cast; and journalistic popularization of the phrase, 'pigeons on the grass alas.' Were the libretto known in a different form it is unthinkable that it could ever have achieved its present celebrity." Bridgman, *Gertrude Stein in Pieces*, 176.
36 Everett Helm, "Virgil Thomson's *Four Saints in Three Acts*," *Music Review* 15 (May 1954), 129.
37 The novelist Jonathan Strong of Somerville, Mass.
38 John McCaffrey, "Any of Mine Without Music to Help Them: The Operas and Plays of Gertrude Stein" *Yale Theatre* 4 (Summer 1973), 39.
39 *New York Times*, 17 November 1934, 13.
40 *The Complete Works of St. Teresa of Jesus*, trans. and ed. E. Allison Peers (London: Sheed and Ward, 1946). See particularly *The Life of the Holy Mother Teresa of Jesus*, Chs. XIX–XXI in Volume I of the *Complete Works*.

41 Robert T. Petersson, *The Art of Ecstasy: Teresa, Bernini and Cra-shaw* (New York: Atheneum, 1970), 11.

42 Ibid.

43 Bridgman, *Gertrude Stein in Pieces,* 180.

44 The magpie is generally taken to be, in a rather crude way, a "symbol" of the Holy Ghost. This reductive reading is traceable to an anecdote Stein recounts in "Plays":

> A very famous French inventor of things that have to do with stabilisation in aviation told me that what I told him magpies did could not be done by any bird but anyway whether the magpies at Avila do do it or do not at least they look as if they do do it. They look exactly like the birds in the Annunciation pictures the bird which is the Holy Ghost and rests flat against the side sky very high. (129)

45 Aside from *The Mother of Us All,* these include *They Must. Be Wed-ded. To Their Wife.*, made a ballet, called *A Wedding Bouquet*, by Lord Gerald Berners; *In Circles* (a retitling of *A Circular Play*), *What Happened*, and an abridgment by Leon Katz of *The Making of Americans,* all set to music by Al Carmines of the Judson Poets' The-ater in New York; *In a Garden*, by Meyer Kupferman; *Ladies' Voices,* by Vernon Martin; *Three Sisters Who Are Not Sisters*, by Ned Rorem; *Photograph — 1920*, by Martin Kalmanoff; *Look and Long*, by Florence Wickham and Marvin Schwartz; *Doctor Faustus Lights the Lights*, by Richard Winslow. See John McCaffrey, "Any of Mine Without Music to Help Them," for descriptions of and information about productions of these. Thomson also set several of Stein's non-dramatic pieces to music: "Susie Asado," "Preciosilla," "Capital Capitals," "Deux Soeurs Qui Ne Sont Pas Soeurs" (the last of these Stein called a "film"). Many of these have been staged by Lawrence Kornfeld.

46 Virgil Thomson, liner notes, recording of *Four Saints in Three Acts* (RCA: 1964), concluding paragraph.

Conclusion

1 Roland Barthes, "Kafka's Answer," *Critical Essays*, trans. Richard Howard (Evanston: Northwestern University Press, 1972), 133.

Index

171

JACKET DESIGNED BY ED FRANK PRODUCTIONS
COMPOSED BY METRICOMP, GRUNDY CENTER, IOWA
MANUFACTURED BY THOMSON-SHORE, INC., DEXTER, MICHIGAN
TEXT AND DISPLAY LINES ARE SET IN PALATINO

Library of Congress Cataloging in Publication Data
DeKoven, Marianne, 1948–
A different language.
Includes bibliographical references and index.
1. Stein, Gertrude, 1874–1946 — Style. 2. Literature,
Experimental. I. Title.
PS3537.T323Z586 1983   818'.5209   82-70558
ISBN 0-299-09210-0